Vaughan Evans is an independent consultant in business strategy and author of many business books, including the bestselling *The Financial Times Essential Guide to Writing a Business Plan*. A Cambridge economics graduate and an Alfred P. Sloan Fellow at London Business School, he worked for many years at management consultants Arthur D. Little and investment bankers Bankers Trust.

Vaughan is also an accomplished speaker. A leading performer on the amateur speaking circuit for twenty-five years, he is well known for the vitality, humour and sheer buzz he injects into every speech.

He has nurtured and mentored dozens of speakers over the years, helping transform hesitant speakers into confident speakers and good speakers into great speakers.

Vaughan hails from West Wales and lives alongside Richmond Park in southwest London. He started his career as a development economist, working for a dozen years in such hardship postings as the British Virgin Islands, Borneo, Fiji, Thailand...! Tales of these travels crop up now and again in his speeches...

PRAISE FOR VAUGHAN EVANS'S PUBLIC SPEAKING ADVICE

'If you think public speaking is an unbreakable code, Vaughan Evans has cracked it! This book fizzes with vitality and oozes valuable advice. Ideal for the starter speaker – and some neat tips too for those further along the road.'

Yvonne Jordan, Interior Designer, Britain and Ireland Champion of Public Speaking, 2012

'This is a zingy, inspiring and practical book . . . It really fired me up – and I learned a lot!'

Cao Jun Cao, PhD researcher, novice speaker

'As a speaker, Vaughan has tremendous charisma and a sense of fun – but he also possesses rich insight into the art of public speaking. Packed with practical tips, advice and wisdom, this book gives you a short-cut to more than 25 years of his public speaking expertise – and wit! Highly recommended, especially to those new to the art.'

Simon Bucknell, speaker, coach, Britain and Ireland Champion of Public Speaking, 2006 & 2007

'Hugely entertaining and thoroughly useful. Reading this book is like watching playback of my favourite comedy show – I can skip, fast forward or rewind at will to a punchline that hits – or bombs! This book is a true gift – a lifetime of wisdom and practical help to anyone who gives a damn about effective communication.'

Lo Luong Lo, Investor, experienced speaker

'This is a smashing read. Vaughan Evans writes as he speaks, with authority, passion and confidence. Read this book and, just as if you were listening to him, you will come away educated, entertained and informed – or you will wake up refreshed!'

Mike Silverman, media executive, former governor of Toastmasters in Britain and Ireland

'Want to stand on stage, frozen rigid, eyes downcast, speaking to the floor, occasionally glancing up to watch the audience yawn? Then don't read this book. If you do, and if you act on just 10% of what's in it, you'll be able to stand, connect, project and, ultimately, deliver.'

Peter Aleksin, stand-up comedian

'The prospect of public speaking can be torturous, intimidating, stomach-churning. Want to know how those emotions can be swept aside? Vaughan Evans offers the breakdown, the solution, the experience of how to stand and deliver. He's a master of the art, and you cannot fail to learn from this brilliant and entertaining breakdown of every potential pitfall. Read and speak!'

Dominic Hart, sports journalist

Other titles

STAND, SPEAK, DELIVER!

Vaughan Evans

ROBINSON

A How To Book

ROBINSON

First published in Great Britain in 2016 by Robinson

Copyright © Vaughan Evans, 2016

The following speeches remain the copyright of the contributors: The Art of Communication (Appendix 1) © Mike Silverman; Just So Lucky (Appendix 2) © Jock Elliott; We Don't Need Another Hero (Appendix 2) © Yvonne Jordan; Accepting the Nobel Prize for Peace (Appendix 3) © His Holiness The Dalai Lama; Reach Your New Year's Goals in Four Easy Steps (Appendix 3) © Brian Tracy; The Iraq Crisis (Appendix 4) © Tony Blair; Europe, One Wink at a Time (Appendix 5) © Laura McCracken; Fruity Cocktails (Appendix 6) © Sonia Aste; Is Money the Root of All Evil? (Appendix 7) © Bill Russell.

1 3 5 7 9 10 8 6 4 2

The moral right of the author has been asserted.

Important note

This book is not an official publication of, nor is it authorised by, Toastmasters International. The advice, tips and opinions in this book are those of the author, unless otherwise specified.

A CIP catalogue record for this book
is available from the British Library.

ISBN: 978-1-47213-580-3 (paperback)

Typeset by Basement Press, Glaisdale
Printed and bound by CPI Group (UK) Ltd, Croydon, CR0 4YY

Papers used by Robinson are from well-managed forests and other responsible sources.

MIX
Paper from
responsible sources
FSC® C104740

Robinson
is an imprint of
Little, Brown Book Group
Carmelite House
50 Victoria Embankment
London EC4Y 0DZ

An Hachette UK Company
www.hachette.co.uk

www.littlebrown.co.uk

How To Books are published by Robinson, an imprint of Little, Brown Book Group. We welcome proposals from authors who have first-hand experience of their subjects. Please set out the aims of your book, its target market and its suggested contents in an email to Nikki.Read@howtobooks.co.uk.

To London Corinthians and other Toastmaster friends.
And to three public speaking charities,
Speakers Trust, Speakers for Schools and IzDaBiz,
to whom author proceeds from this book will be donated.

Speakers Trust (www.speakerstrust.org) is a public speaking training charity which specialises in the education, not-for-profit and community sectors. Its vision is a society where everybody has the skills, confidence and desire to speak in public and its mission is to promote the lifetime benefits of effective public speaking. It has trained over 250,000 people and worked with over 1,000 schools, colleges and charities throughout the UK. Its 'Speak Out! Challenge' for Year 10 pupils is the world's biggest youth speaking event and to date has helped over 100,000 youngsters find their voice.

Speakers for Schools (www.speakers4schools.org) is a charity which provides state secondary schools and colleges with talks from a range of industry leading professionals, public figures and academics, free of charge. Its network consists of 950 speakers who donate their time to go into schools to share their insights and experience through high-profile assembly talks with students. The charity has worked with over 2,000 schools in England, Scotland and Wales.

IzDaBiz is to be a charity which will aim to stimulate interest in business amongst secondary school students. It will use crafted materials to stimulate the students to think for themselves about what makes for a successful business. It will encourage them to consider launching a business as a viable career option and guide them on how to pitch a winning business proposition. It will aim to leave a positive, exciting, can-do impression of business on young minds: business iz da biz…!

CONTENTS

PREFACE: ON THE ORIGINS OF THIS BOOK

I am not a professional speaker, nor a salesman, lecturer or lawyer. I am a consultant in business strategy. With a speaking hobby.

This hobby originated when I stood for Parliament in 1990-92. I figured I knew my party policies well enough, but communicating them in front of an audience of five, twenty, even five hundred was a daunting, even alarming, prospect.

I asked the party. They suggested a course at a college of further education. I went along and sat in a circle around a chap who showed us how to exercise the voice by pulling ridiculous faces and making obscene sounds – which he suggested we practise on the Tube on the way home. I didn't. Nor did I return.

I was despondent, but that very evening my wife came across an advert in the classified pages of a journal which said simply: 'Want to learn how to speak in public? Call now!'. I did. The woman was astonished to hear from me. Mine was the first response to the ad, which had been placed a year beforehand!

Nevertheless, she told me of a public speaking club that had recently opened at a boathouse in Chiswick, West London. Was that anywhere near me, she asked? Near? It was just the other side of the river from me! Was this fate?

I went along to the very next club meeting – and have been going ever since.

As for my political career, the electorate had other ideas. But my hobby had been born. Over the next two and a half decades I spoke frequently at the club, won the major speech contests as often as not and mentored many a member on their speaking journey.

Each year I was asked if I would join the committee and take on the presidency, but I always replied I would do so only when I had enough time to do it justice – once my family had grown up.

Twenty-three years later I took on the role. It requires the delivery of a short, introductory, warm-up talk at the opening of each meeting. I decided to use these mini-speeches to convey, especially to novice speakers, all I had learned along the way about public speaking. Each speech dealt with one facet of speaking. Each speech focused solely on the three or so most important tips about that facet. And, above all, each speech was designed as much to entertain as inform.

Club members enjoyed them – and said they benefited from them – especially the starter speakers.

Some speeches were filmed. You might find them fun and useful too – just punch my name into Google, click on the 'Videos' tab and take a look!

I transcribed the speeches onto the club blog. Members enjoyed reading those too, especially those who were absent at the time.

The blog became this book.

STAND, SPEAK, DELIVER! shares those mini-speeches with you. They are here for your entertainment as much as for your learning. Read this book and you will survive as a speaker. Follow it and you'll thrive!

Enjoy!

INTRODUCTION

ON PUBLIC SPEAKING, PRESENTING AND CONVERSING

What is it about public speaking?

Whether that refers to informing or entertaining a hall full of people or just presenting on your feet to half a dozen colleagues or clients, it ranks in the top ten of people's greatest phobias.

There is even a name for it – glossophobia!

It lurks right up there in many such surveys with the likes of claustrophobia (enclosed spaces), ophidiophobia (snakes) and, as my younger daughter would testify, arachnophobia (spiders).

Behavioural scientists also come up with lists of common human fears, such as pain, loneliness, ridicule, rejection or death. But top of such lists often comes failure.

There may be a connection here. Is glossophobia linked to the fear of failure?

If so, this is an irrational fear. There is no reason why you should fail as a public speaker or presenter. Public speaking is a skill, like driving a car. It can be taught. And it is taught, every day, in books, videos and thousands of public speaking clubs around the world.

Public speaking is essential to progressing our careers, to living our lives fully. If your image of public speaking is one of David Lloyd George on a soapbox, with resplendent wing collar, flowing white locks and impassioned, mellifluous, Celtic oratory, then think again.

Addressing a large audience is but one extreme of public speaking. A much more common situation is the seminar or meeting room, when you are presenting to colleagues or clients. The skills you learn in public speaking are the very same as those you need for presenting.

Learn the skills of public speaking and you will stand out as a presenter.

And what about when you are in a meeting with three, six or a dozen colleagues and your boss turns to you and asks: 'What's your take on this?' If you follow the skills of public speaking, you will answer with a structured 'speech' – with an opening, body and conclusion – and you will deliver your content clearly, coherently and animatedly.

And your answer will be so structured whether you deliver it in three minutes or thirty seconds.

Less obviously, but equally emphatically, the skills of public speaking can be applied to conversing on a one-to-one basis, whether with a friend, acquaintance or colleague. Skills such as varying the voice, using your hands appropriately and keeping the listener entertained will make you an engaging conversationalist.

The best way to improve your public speaking, of course, is to actually do it – to practise, whenever you can, to whatever size of audience.

Or you can observe how others do it – in speeches, whether live or on video.

Here is a new way. Uniquely, this book delivers the essentials of public speaking and presenting in the form of short speeches, thirty-seven of them. Most of these have already been delivered – and videoed – to a live audience by the author, a speaker with a quarter century of experience in speaking – and entertaining.

This is not an in-depth treatise on the subject. It gives you the tips that matter, the ones that make the difference. And it delivers them jovially, wittily and vividly.

Read the book and you will survive as a speaker or presenter.

Follow it and you'll thrive.

ON TOASTMASTERS INTERNATIONAL

I learnt my public speaking skills from an organisation called Toastmasters International. It is a worldwide public speaking club of extraordinary power to enhance people's lives.

It makes hesitant, reticent, even fearful speakers competent. It makes ordinary speakers eloquent, confident and engaging. It makes promising speakers good – and good speakers great.

There are around 15,000 Toastmasters clubs with over 300,000 members in 120+ countries. Of every ten members, five are female, six are in the United States, seven are aged from thirty-five to fifty and eight have a college degree. You can find Toastmasters clubs from Alaska to Alabama, Barbados to Brussels, Costa Rica to China.

I've been a member since 1990, a founder member of London's second oldest club, London Corinthians Toastmasters. Over the years, I've seen scores of people transformed. I've seen petrified speakers learn to control their nerves and ultimately, incredibly, enjoy performing. I've seen dull speakers come alive, good speakers become national champions.

Presentational and public speaking skills are little different from cycling or typing skills. They're not inherited, they can be learned. They're difficult at first to grasp, easy once mastered.

But, unlike cycling skills, which return as soon as you climb back on a bike, public speaking skills are best kept tuned up through regular practice. They are more akin to golfing skills. Stay away from the game for a while and the golf swing develops idiosyncrasies – and your short game goes to pot.

So too in public speaking. The more you do, the more regularly you do it, the sharper you become. Stay away and the rust sets in.

Toastmasters is the ideal forum for such practice. It is a highly structured and mutually supportive environment, with the best learning materials to be found anywhere. Speaker progression is planned, monitored and invariably achieved.

All clubs follow more or less the same format, but most have different nuances, even a distinctive culture (like in my club, where the emphasis has from its creation been one of learning through fun and merriment!).

Find one that suits you, show up every other week and your communication skills will improve, steadily and surely. Irreversibly.

For those readers who aren't members of Toastmasters, let me leave you with this thought. You're reading a book on public speaking. There's no more effective programme for public speaking worldwide than Toastmasters International. Type the word Toastmasters and the name of your town or county into Google, find the nearest club, and go along as a guest. You have nothing to lose.

You'll come across a bunch of like-minded souls. At worst, you'll have a good evening's entertainment. For free.

At best, it'll transform your life.

INITIATION

I was late, of course. I poked my head through the door and this tall, fine-looking, elegant woman standing at the front of a group of twenty or so people spotted me and instantly let loose a warm, Southern US, sing-song greeting: 'Hiiiii, you must be Vaaaaan?' 'That's me,' I responded. 'Waaaeeell, welcome to Toastmasters!', she enthused – and the whole room burst into applause! Just for walking through the door! I almost did an about-turn. Had I stumbled upon an undercover branch of Alcoholics Anonymous?

Fifteen minutes later I was on my feet, asked to deliver a one-and-a-half minute impromptu speech. I had been given a peach of a topic, 'a holiday misadventure'. I spoke about how I had been robbed at knife-point in a Colombian hostel in the 1970s. I can talk for an hour or more on that story, riddled with embellishment, of course. But I dried up completely after forty-five seconds and could think of no more to say. I returned to my seat, head bowed, in abject shame.

Yet the whole room applauded – again! Wow, I thought, that feels better. I felt the warmth, I felt the support, the empathy.

> I wanted to get back up there, to show them I could do better
> next time. I wanted to justify their faith in me.
> This clap-clap approach seemed to work!
>
> —Vaughan Evans (extract from a 10th anniversary speech to
> London Corinthians Toastmasters, 2000)

HOW TO USE THIS BOOK

This book serves three purposes. It gives key tips on how to construct and deliver a speech or presentation. It demonstrates how a speech should be structured and balanced. And it seeks to entertain.

This is no academic treatise or tome on public speaking. There are plenty of them around. This book gives you *the essentials* of public speaking, the most important tips the author has picked up from years of experience and has passed on to members of his public speaking club.

All you need to know on how to survive as a speaker or presenter is in here. The book is in five parts:

- *Preparing to speak or present* – find out who's going to be in the audience, dress for the part, choose the right topic, decide which speaking aids to use, if any
- *Structuring the speech or presentation* – give it an opening, body and conclusion, stick up signposts throughout, build in some light relief, bring in some of yourself, deploy words out of the common and perhaps illustrate with props

- *Delivering the speech or presentation* – make sure you get the basics right (stand and deliver, look us in the eye, come alive!), conquer the fear, vary the voice, move the body and interact with the audience
- *Speaking with purpose* – for instance for purposes of information, humour, entertainment, inspiration, motivation, persuasion, Best Man . . .
- *Presenting* – use the above tips from public speaking, plus a few special to presenting, and you will stand head and shoulders above your fellow presenters at work

Each speech restricts its tips to just a few, often with a three-letter acronym for ease of memory retention. I hope these are not overdone, but the whole purpose of the book is to get you up and running as a public speaker – and you don't want to have to memorise an encyclopaedia to get there.

You can dip in and out of these parts or chapters as you see fit. The book can be read straight through or as needed.

ON ACRONYMS

At the end of my term as president of my Toastmasters club, I was subject to the customary, if cumulatively brutal, presidential roasting over dinner at a pub in London's Pimlico. One such roaster, Lo, mocked my perhaps obsessive use of acronyms for my speaking tips, like how one should try and BED the audience in a persuasive speech (see Speech 29).

On the plus side, she sandwiched her roast by saying that my presidency had also contained plenty of energy, vitality and banter. In short, it had been scintillating, obsessive and buzzy: SOB. Neat!

The second purpose is to *demonstrate* how a speech should be structured and balanced. This is done very simply, by wrapping all the essential tips into thirty-seven speeches. Observe how each speech is structured by using the template of opening, body and conclusion, and that structure should be well and truly ingrained in your psyche by the end of the book!

But the book also shows you how to balance your speech. There is a fine line between a speech and a lecture (see Speech 8). It is best to assume that the audience has a limited time span for taking in information. Many lecturers ignore this. Better lecturers build in a break every so often. The best lecturers, and all speakers, should look for an element of light relief in every paragraph – or, at the outside, every other paragraph – unless, it goes without saying, the speech is of a very serious or sad nature.

Light relief is shown in this book by the use of *bold italics*. Sometimes it is a quote, or it may be an anecdote or a gag. Hopefully you'll find these elements of relief stimulating and amusing. Others will bomb. It doesn't matter – even stinkers have the effect of breaking up the flow, lightening the atmosphere, enabling the listener (or reader) to shift from one buttock to the other.

And if a yarn or quip does founder, you can use that for *more* light relief, for example, with this: 'Well, that one fell on stony ground. My mate Jack Dee* asked me to try it out for him. *Thanks a lot, Jack!'*

---

* Or another well-known comedian appropriate to the style of the dud gag!

ACKNOWLEDGEMENTS

This book would not have been possible without my having been a member of Toastmasters International since 1990, and in particular of the extraordinary club that is London Corinthians. Here the culture is one of learning through fun and merriment, the famed Corinthians' 'buzz'. It has been a highlight of my every fortnight for three decades.

I can therefore be regarded fairly as a product of the club. As such, any wayward tip in this book, any linguistic shortcoming and, especially, any gag that bombs, let alone makes the skin crawl, should be regarded as the responsibility, solely, indubitably and indisputably, of the club, in accordance with the jurisdiction of the Court of Llareggub*.

Which brings us to the final purpose of the book – to entertain as much as to inform. Most of these speeches were performed to a live audience and they seemed to do just that – allowing for the odd bomb, or a hundred. Feedback by readers of the transcripts on the club's blog was also positive and encouraging.

I hope you too find the speeches both informative and entertaining. If not, don't blame the book. As Groucho Marx observed: 'Outside of a dog, a book is a man's best friend. ***Inside a dog, it's too hard to read.***'

Enjoy!

---

* If you don't get this reference, shame on you! But, fear not, better late than never – grab a copy of Dylan Thomas's *Under Milk Wood* sometime soon and bask in the glow of a master wordsmith!

OPENING

1

THE ULTIMATE SECRET TO PUBLIC SPEAKING IS . . . !

Mr Chairman, ladies and gentlemen, what is the answer to the ultimate question of life, the universe and everything? Yes, forty-two – according to Douglas Adams in his *Hitchhiker's Guide to the Galaxy*.

But he was misguided. It is public speaking! Public speaking is the key that opens so many doors of opportunity in life. The US comedian Milton Berle once said: *'If opportunity doesn't knock, build a door!'* Fine, but what do you say when the doorman opens it? *That's public speaking!*

What then is the answer to the ultimate question of life, the universe and public speaking? Here is my shortlist of three:

- Structure your speech or presentation with an opening, body and conclusion
- Look the audience in the eye
- Speak with passion

Sure, they are all important, but which is the most important of these three? Hands up those who think it is 'structure your speech'. And those who think it is 'look the audience in the eye'. And 'speak with passion'?

Ladies and gentlemen, I agree/disagree with the majority. The ultimate secret of public speaking is to speak with passion on a subject about which you feel passionate. It will transform your speaking style, whether you are new to public speaking or a seasoned old pro like me. Your whole persona will radiate emotion and enthusiasm and that will infect and suck in the audience.

We Celts have a word for this, *hwyl*. There is no direct translation but it conjures up the kind of passion, spirit and fervour which rouses the individual and collective purpose. They say it is worth 10 points at every match in the Millennium Stadium, Cardiff. Think of Martin Luther King speaking with *hwyl* about racial equality. In scary contrast, ponder Adolf Hitler speaking just as passionately, and, tragically, just as rousingly, about racial hatred. Or look at Homer Simpson when he speaks passionately of his family. He meets an alien and says: 'Please don't eat me, I have a wife and three kids. ***Eat them!***'

That's another secret, by the way. Stick a slug of humour into (almost) every speech or presentation. But we'll come to that another day. First things first, hit it with *hwyl*. Tony Robbins says that 'passion is the genesis of genius'. Oscar Wilde said to a customs official at the port of New York: ***'I have nothing to declare but my genius!'*** Declare *your* genius, ladies and gentlemen, speak with ***fiery, flaming, brimstone-burning passion!***

Mr Chairman

PART I:
PREPARING TO SPEAK OR PRESENT

2

KNOW YOUR AUDIENCE: WHO ARE THEY?

Mr Chairman, ladies and gentlemen, have you ever stood up in front of an audience, taken a look round and thought to yourself: OMG, what am I doing here? These people are not what I expected. They don't look very friendly. In the immortal words of Butch Cassidy: [COWBOY ACCENT] *who are these guys?*

It happened to me in my very early days of public speaking. I was fortunate enough to win this club's very first Humorous Speech contest in 1990 with a speech full of anecdotes about some of the wonderful characters I used to live amongst on the small Caribbean island of Tortola in the mid-1970s. Parts of the speech were delivered in my best [JAMAICAN ACCENT] *Jaameeacan accent, maan!* The next round was the area contest. At the time, there were only two clubs in London, three in the commuter belt and one in a market town which shall remain nameless, right down on the South coast – which is where the area contest was held.

I duly showed up and the atmosphere was so alien I could have been on Mars. My own club was a mélange of different nationalities, ages and sexes. In this charming corner of Little England, it was overwhelmingly male, middle-aged plus and English. Tea and cakes were served on arrival and *the hosts all had their pinkies out*! My rather raunchy speech, which had inspired many a hearty guffaw at the club contest, was heard *in silence*. My Jamaican accent was greeted with *polite puzzlement*. The whole performance was excruciatingly inappropriate to *an audience of waxworks*!

Ladies and gentlemen, the first rule of preparing any speech or presentation is to know your audience. Who's there? As in: Knock, knock. Who's there? Jamaica. Jamaica who? ***Jamaica me crazy wid all dem knack knack jokes!***

A little bit of preparation is all it takes – an email or two, a phone call, a few minutes on the internet. Who will be there? What age group? What sex? What educational level? What cultural sensitivities? If yours is a business talk, what managerial level will they be? Will they be there voluntarily or under instructions? Are they expecting to be educated or entertained – or both?

There used to be a guideline at our club that talking about sex, religion and politics was taboo. This was always a bit of a puzzle: ***what else was there to speak about***? So we wrote to Toastmasters International HQ and obtained further guidance. The answer was rather sensible: speeches containing references to sex, religion or politics should be mindful of the sensitivities of the audience. Fair enough. In other words, know your audience. So, graphic re-enactments of romantic episodes are out – I kid you not, we had a speech at this club a few years ago where a speaker gave us the full works, ***pelvic thrusts, grunts, shrieks, the lot***! It was cringingly embarrassing and grotesquely out of order.

In summary, ladies and gentlemen, the first rule of preparing to speak is to know your audience. Having been a member of this club for twenty-three years, I hope by now I know this audience. Or, should I say: [JAMAICAN ACCENT] ***maan, dis aa'dience be . . . irie!***

Mr Cheeair . . . maan!

3

LOOKING THE PART: GET TOGGED UP!

[ENTER IN FLORAL WAISTCOAT, HEADBAND AND SHADES, ADOPT WEST COAST HIPPIE ACCENT] *Do you dig my gear, man?* [NORMAL ACCENT] Appropriate for the occasion, would you say? Conveying authority, dignity, credibility? Presidential? Perhaps not!

[TOSS AWAY WAISTCOAT, HEADBAND AND SHADES, PULL ON BLAZER] Now, how about that? *Am I your president again?*

Madam Chairman, ladies and gentlemen, there is one golden rule on how to dress when you speak in public. It is this. Be as well dressed as the best dressed person in the room. If you don't look the part, you're starting off your speech on the back foot. You'll have to fight extra hard to gain the audience's credibility. Public speaking can be hard enough as it is. Why make it harder?

There are exceptions, of course. If my speech this evening was going to be about my days as a hippie wannabe in the late 1960s, my dress might have been just the ticket. I would have been using my attire as a prop. So for example if you wish to give a speech on the sexualisation of society, you may choose, Carol*, to wear your dress as a prop, *with a plunging neckline and heaving cleavage*. [PAUSE] *Please!*

I got it very wrong the other day. The parents' association at my son's school organised a Burns Night, but it was called off at the

---

* Note: A well-endowed lady in the audience, of a certain age and known to be a good sport!

last moment due to heavy snow. So they rearranged it to coincide with St David's Day five weeks later and invited me along too, as a token Welsh parent. I was asked if I'd like to sing a song or tell a tale. *I opted for both!*

I showed up a bit late and found the school hall full of stern-faced men in dinner jackets and kilts. I was wearing a blazer with an open-necked shirt. Oops! I had never received the original Burns Night invitation and hadn't got round to asking about dress code. But I needn't have worried. This was a Scottish do and very soon [SCOTS ACCENT] *the golden nectarrrr was flowing*. By the time I got up it had started to work its magic, and those formerly pale faces were now distinctly ruddier. *I was saved by the Bells!*

In summary, ladies and gentlemen, a public speaker – or presenter – needs to look the part. Play it safe: be as well dressed as the best dressed person in the room. In other words [PUT HEADBAND BACK ON AND BRING BACK HIPPIE ACCENT], *get decked out like funky, groovy, heavy . . . chicks and cats*!

Madam Chairman

4

CHOOSING THE TOPIC: LIGHT YOUR FIRE!

Madam Chairman, ladies and gentlemen, I would like to say a few words this evening about . . . [PAUSE, THEN ANNOUNCE EXTRAVAGANTLY, AS IN BINGO HALL] *double-entry bookkeeping! Did I hear a groan?* Why?! Many accountants get very excited about double-entry bookkeeping. They go to double-entry conferences, double-entry seminars, maybe even to double-entry parties – which sounds like something out of *Fifty Shades of Grey*! *Now you're interested . . . !*

There are two basic guidelines in choosing a topic to speak about. First it should be one that the audience can relate to – one that is going to interest them, or inform them, educate them, entertain them, persuade them, even inspire them.

But best of all is to find a topic that you feel strongly about, one that evokes the passion in you. Something that lights your fire. [SING] *Light my fire, light my fire, light my fire . . . !*

I remember a speech in this club maybe seven, eight years ago. It was given by a lovely lady, quiet, diffident, single, in her early fifties. She had been with the club a couple of years and, if truth be told, hers weren't the liveliest of speeches. She was difficult to hear, due to her shyness and soft, heavily accented delivery, and she tended to choose safe topics that didn't seem to inspire her, let alone the audience.

Her final speech at the club was on a different planet. She announced that she had sold her flat, she was leaving London and returning to her native Glasgow. She shared with us her intention, her vow, to dedicate the rest of her life to saving the Scots language – the language of Scottish kings prior to union with England, the tongue of [SCOTS ACCENT] ***Rrrrrrrabbie Burrrrrrrns***. She was so passionate about her native language that her face, her body, her persona became transformed, her voice too – we could hear her every word, we could *feel* her every word. Tears came to our eyes and we all rose as one to our feet when she finished. It was a truly emotional, cathartic moment for her and for us all, a privilege to be there.

Speaking from the heart does wonders for you. You won't worry about what you're going to say, no problem if you lose your way, because you can talk for days on your passion. You won't need notes. You will come alive, radiate, be as one with the audience.

So, ladies and gentlemen, choose a topic that will appeal to the audience, by all means, but better still choose one that lights your fire – ***as long as it's not double-entry bookkeeping***!

Madam Chairman

5

USING SPEAKING AIDS: REMEMBER THE 3RS!

Mr Chairman, ladies and gentlemen, who here feels more comfortable speaking with some sort of aid to hand – notes, flipchart, PowerPoint? Come on, be honest! Yes, it is most of us. Not you, George? You prefer the freedom of the stage, you like to wing it? Aah, if only the world had more Georges in it . . . *On second thoughts . . . !*

The truth is that most of us are petrified of losing our way, forgetting our lines. I've been at this game for almost a quarter of a century and last year represented this club in the area contest, giving exactly the same speech I had given at the club contest two weeks earlier. After five minutes, I drew a blank. I had no idea what came next and had to sit down. Pathetic, really – and I can't even put it down to age. I remember doing the same thing once fifteen years or so ago. It just happens.

In the real world, beyond the bubble of a speaking club, you just can't do that. The show must go on. Whether you are speaking at a conference, to a society or a charity, or presenting to a room full of colleagues or clients, your audience is relying on you. They may even be paying for you to get to the finishing line. Most of us need some help with that.

By far the best is to have a handful of plain postcards with you, each with just three or four bullets, each bullet with just three or four words, in capitals. Like this. [SHOW CARDS] These words are an aide-mémoire, no more. Don't have the whole speech on a lectern with you, just the postcards. Or hold them instead in your left hand, freeing your right hand for gestures.

If you feel the audience would benefit from visuals, use either a flipchart or PowerPoint. Note that I said visuals. The audience doesn't want to see interminable sentences on the screen – just simple charts, images or, if you must, bulleted headings – again, a maximum three or four words for each bullet. Don't do as in the famous Dilbert cartoon: he is standing in front of a screen with a slide which is completely black. He explains that his boss has told him he didn't want too many bullet points. 'So,' says Dilbert, *'I gave him one, a long one!'*

No matter whether you use notes, flipcharts or PowerPoint, however, there are three golden rules: the 3Rs. Read, Reset, Release. Do not speak while you are looking down, across or, worst of all, at the screen behind you. [BACK TO AUDIENCE] Can you hear me? Maybe, but even if you have a loud voice like me, you will not be communicating with the audience. [TURN TO FRONT] <u>Read</u> the notes, <u>reset</u> your eyes on the audience then <u>release</u> your words – in that order.

That reminds me of my favourite Sergeant-Major joke. [SERGEANT-MAJOR VOICE AGAIN] 'Attenshuuun! Smith, I didn't see your miserable personage at camouflage training this morning.' *'Thank you, sir!'*

So, in summary, ladies and gentlemen, by all means use notes and visual aids in the real world. But make them short and punchy – and never read directly from them. Instead use the 3Rs: Read, Reset and Release! In other words, [SERGEANT MAJOR STYLE COMMAND] *eyes . . . FRONT!*

Mr Chairman

TOP TEN DOS AND DON'TS IN PREPARING TO SPEAK OR PRESENT . . . NOT!

- **Do** your own thing – don't worry about who's in the audience

- **Do** be smutty – if Mrs Grundy doesn't approve, she has issues

- **Do** wear what you want – Bermuda shorts to a black tie do, why not?

- **Do** use text on PowerPoint – and the more the merrier

- **Do** focus on your notes – we don't want to see your eyes

- **Don't** crack a joke – we are here to be informed, not entertained

- **Don't** speak from the heart – that's just sentimental

- **Don't** choose a topic that interests the audience – we love to yawn

- **Don't** worry about remembering your lines – you can always ad lib . . .

- **Don't** use pictures on PowerPoint – they're for kiddies

PART II:
CRAFTING THE SPEECH
OR PRESENTATION

6

STRUCTURING THE SPEECH I: TOP AND TAIL IT!

Mr Chairman, ladies and gentlemen, *'To begin at the beginning: it is spring, moonless night in the small town, starless and bible-black, the cobblestreets silent, and the hunched, courters'-and- rabbits' wood limping invisible down to the sloeblack, slow, black, crowblack, fishingboat-bobbing sea.'*

Isn't that the most magical opening in the history of English literature? They are, of course, the words of Dylan Thomas, in his play for voices, *Under Milk Wood*. Every book benefits from an emphatic opening, and so too does every speech. Indeed a speech structure is a simple affair: an opening (think of the head), a conclusion (the feet) and in the middle a body, preferably [INDICATE] ***tightly honed!***

The body is where the bulk of your speech goes – in a seven-minute speech, plan on five minutes of body, with one minute each for the opening and the conclusion. These are the most important parts of any speech, the topping and the tailing. The opening should grab the attention of the audience. The conclusion should ensure that the speech lingers in the memory.

Openings should be dramatic – you should try and start with a bang. Here are some ideas: you could try a quote, as I did this evening. Or you could ask the audience a stimulating question, even a loaded one such as '***How many of you here this evening have stopped watching internet porn?*** [PULL DOWN HAND, PUT IT UP AGAIN, DOWN AGAIN, THROW HANDS IN THE AIR, AT A LOSS!] That usually livens up the audience!

Or you could sing a song – as I once did on a speech on setting goals. I opened with some Rolling Stones: [SING] 'No, you can't always get what you want . . . ' Whereupon some wag piped up with: *'Not surprising, with a voice like that . . . '*

Most important of all is the conclusion. That's what people are going to take away from your speech or presentation. If it's a contest, that's what the judges will remember. If it is a pitch to clients, that is what they will recall. So here's a tip: whether your speech is a seven-minute standard, a one-minute impromptu or a forty-minute keynote, save your best to the last.

If it's a persuasive speech, conclude with a call to action. If it's an educational speech, ram home the key message. If it's a humorous speech, keep your best gag in the bag until the end. Now I am seriously setting myself up for a fall here, but here we go . . . !

In summary, ladies and gentlemen, you should structure your speech with a dramatic opening, a well-honed body and a memorable conclusion. Talking of the ultimate conclusion, the end of the world, if that should happen tomorrow, I know where I would like to be – back in the town of my birth, Aberystwyth, on the West coast of Wales, the far side of the Cambrian mountains. *Everything takes at least ten years to get there.*

Mr Chairman

7

STRUCTURING THE SPEECH II: GUIDE US, O!

Madam Chairman, ladies and gentlemen, [SING] 'Guide me, O thou great redeemer . . . ' I know, **any excuse for a Welshman to open his vocal cords . . .** !

But, would you believe, those words are actually relevant to my theme this evening – **well, sort of**! I want to talk about guidance. Last time we met I talked about structuring a speech, how each speech should have an emphatic, perhaps dramatic opening and a memorable, perhaps rousing finale. Now let's address the bit in the middle, the body.

This is the meat of a speech or presentation. It is where the real content lies. It should best be sliced into two, three or four sections. Best of all is three – psychologists have proven that human beings can best process things in threes. They call it 'the power of three'.

But most important are the connections between these sections – what is called 'signposting'. There is a standard old maxim in speaking and presenting: tell us what you are going to tell us, tell us and then tell us what you told us. It has a dual advantage: the audience is given guidance on where you are and where you're going <u>and</u> it reinforces your message. Let me give you an example: suppose I am giving a speech on why, in this feminist-dominated world, **we men still have our uses**.

I could open my speech with, say, a song: [SING] **'It's raining men . . .'** Then I could move into the body by saying we men still have our uses and here are three: we tend to the garden, we take out the rubbish and, in comparison to the alternative of artificial insemination, *we make the act of procreation more aerobically beneficial*.

I then go into detail on how useful we are in the garden. Well, it's best to keep us away from tending the flower bed, but *we are quite good at stuffing the compost heap*. Once I finish that section, I say: we men are useful not only in the garden, but in the house too, like in taking out the rubbish. Well, we can't be bothered with all this recycling business, a box for this, a bag for that, but *we are quite good at stuffing the rubbish bin*. Once I'm done with that, I say: we've seen how indispensable we men are in the garden and in the house, but there's *one final area where we can put to good use our talents at stuffing . . .*

In summary, ladies and gentlemen, carve up the body of your speech or presentation into three and [SING AGAIN] *'Guide us, O . . . '* with signposts. Let me end on a personal note. I must confess I am pretty hopeless in the garden and I moan incessantly about sorting out the rubbish, but, with regard to the third area of male usefulness, *I do offer complimentary evening classes . . . !*

Madam Chairman

8

LIGHTENING THE SPEECH: GIVE US A BREAK!

Mr Chairman, ladies and gentlemen, I would like to talk to you this evening about the profession of accountancy and why you might seriously consider it as a career option. It offers stable employment, a comfortable standard of living and, above all, it trains its members to become the world's best . . . *lovers*!

This is of course no secret! It has been known for two and a half thousand years, ever since Brahmin priests first published a book on love, the Kama Sutra. There they advised that the secret to the art of love was to keep the woman happy. And the best way to do that was for the man to count to 1,000 . . . *and who better to do that than an accountant*?!

There are two main reasons why you should use humour in almost every speech or presentation – even one on accountancy, *especially one on accountancy*! Your audience needs it. And you need it.

First, your audience needs it. Scientists have measured the human *attention* span at forty-nine minutes. But that says nothing about the human *enjoyment* span. In my experience, that is measured at around one, maximum two minutes. We need a break, a laugh, an anecdote, virtually every paragraph – *unless* your speech is a sad or poignant one. Without the light relief, your speech runs the risk of becoming a lecture. And you know the definition of a lecture: *when the audience becomes anaesthetised at both ends*!

And <u>you</u> need it. Humour transforms the speaker. It makes you come alive – the eyes twinkle, the voice gets more vital, the face more expressive, the hands more activated, the body more mobile. You become a more engaging speaker. The audience will warm to you and your message will be communicated more effectively. Think of Boris and Dave. Who would you prefer to listen to? Love him or loathe him, Boris is a character. The other day he strode into his office in the Glass Gonad, decked out in his cycle helmet, looking full of himself, as usual, and announced 'I now have my own Boris bike!', whereupon his secretary burst into tears, sobbing, *'I do have a name, you know!'*

Ooh, that didn't go down too well. Sorry, ladies. [ADDRESS WOMAN IN FRONT ROW] It could have been worse though, madam. *You could have been an accountant too!* You are? *Help!*

So, in summary, try and inject some humour into (almost) every speech or presentation. Your audience craves it. And you need it. *Especially if you are an accountant!* By the way, do you know the main reason why someone decides to pursue a career as an accountant? *When they realise they don't have the charisma to make it as an undertaker!*

Mr Chairman

9

PERSONALISING THE SPEECH: TELL US OF YOU!

Madam Chairman, ladies and gentlemen, last time we met, I told you a tall tale* about when I sang one line of a song and the final note pierced the back wall of this room, shattered a chandelier in the bar and set off a string of extraordinary consequences. That tale was greeted *with rumbustious applause – in my dreams*!

But suppose I had started the speech with, say, Katherine Jenkins singing that note, instead of me – a more attractive vision, for sure, and perhaps more credible, since it tends to be the soprano voice that cracks glass rather than a bass voice. But would the speech have been as well received?

I would suggest not. Personalising a speech makes it more relevant to the audience, more immediate. It helps engage the audience. It invites empathy.

And not just in a humorous speech, but in any speech. Think back a couple of months to Margaret's story on life under Nazi occupation in Poland. That tragic story would have moved us however it was structured, but it was made doubly moving by how Margaret personalised it. She told us the story through the construct of her father telling her the story. She told us that it was the first time that her father had ever spoken to her about life under the Nazis. And the last. Margaret personalised the story and it touched our hearts.

Here's another example. Last meeting Vicky gave us a speech on CDOs, a.k.a. collateralised debt obligations. *There's a winning topic!* It was a brave effort, delivered in her usual effervescent style, but there was no getting away from it – it was about an esoteric financial instrument of no interest to the vast majority of us. One way she might have enlivened the speech would have been to personalise it. She could perhaps have invented a story about how she joined the bank in the first place *because she was a chocaholic*. She had heard that the bank was the European leader in CDOs – and she thought these were a variant, a derivative even, of CDMs. *CDMs, anyone? Yes, Cadbury's Dairy Milk!* That's a cumbersome 1960s anecdote, chosen deliberately, of course – to show that a lousy anecdote is often better than no anecdote at all. It gives the audience a break.

So, ladies and gentlemen, whatever the speech, whether serious or humorous, even perhaps in a presentation to colleagues or clients, think about personalising it. Build yourself into the story. Be yourself. In the words of this club's phantom patron, Oscar Wilde: *Be yourself – everyone else is already taken!*

Madam Chairman

---

* Speech 26

10

ENLIVENING THE SPEECH: HAM IT UP!

Mr Chairman, ladies and gentlemen, *welcome to the wonderful world of words*! There, right there, in one phrase, we capture two important aspects of public speaking. To speak is to utter words – so let's use them well. And all four of the main words in the phrase started with a 'w' – alliteration, one of the main tools of the trade for building a memorable speech.

William Shakespeare, history's wordsmith par excellence, gave these lines to Troilus: 'Words, words, mere words, no matter from the heart'. But I have quoted out of context. No one knew better than Shakespeare the power of words to convey and imprint a message.

Here are three tips on working with words: the power of three, word pictures and tools of the trade. But, before I get going, here's a very quick word on using redundant, space-filling, irritating words like actually, basically or literally: *Don't*!

First, the power of three. Research has shown that people can retain and be influenced by three points but no more. This applies just as well to descriptive adjectives, adverbs or phrases. Thus when telling us a tale about when you met your first love, don't just say 'she was so beautiful'. Tell us instead she was 'sparkling, radiant and *transcended any previous perception of beauty*'. A bit flowery, perhaps, but then *I am a Celt*!

Second, create word pictures. Help the audience to visualise where you are in your story. Don't just say you walked nervously into the office for an interview. Tell us about walking in trepidation into that *'sparse, antiseptic, soul-devouring space'*. Don't just say you went for a pint in the pub. Tell us how you crawled into that *'dank, gloomy, sawdust-trodden drinking den'*. Don't just tell us that you sunbathed on the beach. Tell us how you luxuriated on that *'palm-bedecked, quartz-sparkling, Venus-reclining beach'*. *Getting a bit carried away here . . . !*

Finally, the tools of the trade. Again, there are loads of tools. But, let's face it, we're not all English scholars, so let's stick to the three basics – the power of three again – hyperbole, alliteration and metaphors (or similes). That's HAM, or ham – in other words, *imagine you're hamming it up on stage*! So don't just tell us you were 'excited' at your achievement, tell us you were 'over the moon' – that's a hyperbole and a metaphor, all in one. Want to go one further? Build in some alliteration and tell us you were 'over the moon, that *magical, mystical, miraculous moon'*!

Ladies and gentlemen, don't just speak to us with plain words. Work with them. Play with them. HAM them up. You can even try and make them funny, seriously funny – *that's an oxymoron, by the way . . . !*

Mr Chairman

11

ILLUSTRATING THE SPEECH: USE 'EM PROP'LY!

Madam Chairman, ladies and gentlemen, do you like my presidential medallion? Does it give me added authority? *Do I need that extra gravitas? Yes? That's not the answer I was looking for!*

This medallion is effectively a prop. I have given or listened to hundreds of speeches over the last twenty-three years and the vast majority haven't used props. They haven't needed to. *Nor does this speech!* [REMOVE MEDALLION AND TOSS IT AWAY!]

That is rule number one about a prop. Only use it for a purpose, if it really adds colour to a speech or the speaker. The correct prop can bring a speech to life. Instead of using word pictures in your speech, you can show us real images. Or the real thing – an object we can see, even touch. If your speech is on how you like to vary your headgear depending on your mood, as was a hilarious speech by Celia in the mid-1990s, come armed with a boxful of hats – in her case, more than a dozen of them! If you're going to give a speech on skydiving, come dressed, as did Tanya a couple of years ago, in a parachute harness! *If, ladies, you're going to give a speech on your recent holiday at the naturist resort . . . !*

The second rule is not to let the prop get in the way of the message. It is there to support your speech not to dictate it. Don't use too many and don't let it be unwieldy or take too much time to set up. I remember Graham's speech a few years ago on puppetry – unfortunately all the strings got tangled up and the puppet became totally disorientated. Brilliantly, he improvised. He switched to ventriloquism: *'Well, you've been a useless audience, so I'm going home!'* He threw the puppet into the corner and walked off the stage – and won the contest!

In summary, ladies and gentlemen, do think about using props – but only if they serve a purpose and as long as they don't muddy the message. As for me, if I needed a prop to give me added authority, I wouldn't use a medallion, *I'd use the real thing*! [PULL OUT A WATER PISTOL FROM JACKET AND SQUIRT THE FRONT ROW!]

Madam Chairman

TOP TEN DOS AND DON'TS IN CRAFTING THE SPEECH OR PRESENTATION . . . NOT!

- **Do** go your own way in the body of the speech – we'll catch up soon enough

- **Do** take your speech seriously – this is no occasion for frivolity

- **Do** stick to the facts and the analysis – we're not interested in you

- **Do** use simple language – flamboyant words are for show-offs

- **Do** have props to hand – any are better than none

- **Don't** waste time with signposting – that's dull and repetitive

- **Don't** be dramatic in your opening – that's for drama queens

- **Don't** contrive a conclusion – just end your speech politely

- **Don't** use figures of speech – metaphors confuse

- **Don't** fret when setting up a complicated prop – we can wait

PART III:
DELIVERING THE SPEECH OR PRESENTATION

12

APPLYING THE BASICS: IT S AS EASY AS ABC!

Mr Chairman, ladies and gentlemen. OK, you've done all the necessary preparation. You've written a well-structured speech or presentation. Now it's time to deliver. A hundred dos and don'ts are rushing around your head. Do this, don't do that – oh, yes, and remember the lines!

Relax. Apply the basics. It's as easy as ABC. A is to anchor, to stand firm on the stage. B is to be bold, look the audience in the eye. And C is to come alive! Let's take one at a time.

A is to anchor. Stand and deliver. Not too far back, not too close. Just a pace or two from the front row. Stand with one foot in front of the other. This gives you plenty of flexibility to move forward for emphasis. Don't stand with your legs apart – that is too rigid and restricts your movement. It also acts as a barrier to communication with the audience: it says *I'm a tough mother, don't mess with me*!

B is to be bold. Look the audience in the eye. That way you establish a connection with the audience AND the audience can hear you. In particular, look someone in the back row in the eye. Talk to that person and the whole room will hear you. Then move on to someone else and talk directly to them. Work the audience over with a zig-zag. Don't talk to the floor, nor to the ceiling. Talk to individual members of the audience, one at a time. As Virgil said: *'Fortune favours the bold.'*

C is to come alive. Think of yourself as an electrical gadget. Turn on the switch and your eyes, your face, your voice, your whole body become energised. You come alive. Hopefully you have chosen a speech topic about which you are passionate. Let that passion show. In the words of Howard Thurman: 'Don't ask what the world needs. Ask what makes you come alive, and go do it. *Because what the world needs is people who have come alive.*'

Now let's see the difference. First, let me do the opposite of the ABC, the XYZ perhaps of public speaking – I am standing way back, looking at the floor and [MONOTONICALLY] *speaking like a dalek*. Now let me apply the ABC basics of public speaking – I am anchored up front, looking boldly into your eyes and [VIBRANTLY] I am coming alive.

Ladies and gentlemen, [WITH PIZZAZZ] *it's show time!*

Mr Chairman

13

CONQUERING THE FEAR: FEED LIKE PAC MAN!

Madam Chairman, ladies and gentlemen. Do we have any guests this evening? You are most welcome. You, sir, in the second row, would you please rise to your feet? Thank you. How do you feel? A little apprehensive? No? Just my luck, I choose the only person in the house who is super-cool! That's fine, you can sit down now, sir!

I've got good news and bad news for you. First the bad: I've been speaking for twenty-three years and the fear is still there, not very different from what it was on Day One. That tightening in the pit of the stomach as we rise to speak, it never disappears. Now the good: being nervous is good for speaking, it builds adrenaline and helps sharpen up your act. You just need to control it and work around it.

There are three ways you can conquer that fear. Practising, Attracting and Chilling. PAC. You too can be Pac-Man. Who remembers Pac-Man? Yeah! Like Pac-Man, you can feed on your fear, one Pac-dot at a time.

First, practising. I have heard people say that public speaking is like riding a bike. Learn how to do it and you're away. Alas, it's not quite that simple. Speaking requires regular practice. It's more like the golf swing. Stay away from the game for a while and all sorts of faults can creep in. [DEMONSTRATE . . .] You might take the club back with your hands not your body. You might hit from the top. You might pull your head up too soon. Same in speaking, but the good news is that it is not as unforgiving as golf. Get just the one thing wrong in the golf swing and you're stuffed. The ball will fly off anywhere. Get one thing wrong in speaking and your speech won't be great, but you shouldn't be stuffed.

That reminds me of a former boss who, shamefully, was a keen hunter, including big game. One Monday this magnificent stuffed lion appeared in the office reception area. 'Wow,' I asked her, 'did you shoot that?' 'Sure, last summer,' she replied proudly, 'when my husband and I were on safari at the Kruger.' 'What did you stuff it with?' *'My ex-husband!'*

But there is no substitute for practising. Think of stand-up comics – very little is impromptu, virtually every line is scripted and rehearsed a hundred times. You need not do the same. There is no need to remember every word – the odd stutter or stumble makes a speech seem more authentic. But it is best to memorise your opening – that'll help calm your nerves as you get going. Practice makes perfect, they say. In the words of Woody Allen: *'The reason I became such a good lover is that I practiced a lot on my own.'*

Second, attracting. No, you don't have to look like Angelina or Brad. But it does help to smile. If you smile, you attract the audience onto your side. And their encouragement will make you feel more wanted, less nervous. Think on George Eliot: *'Wear a smile and have friends; wear a scowl and have wrinkles.'*

Finally, chilling. Don't rush your speech. Enjoy being on stage. Relax, take your time, build in plenty of pauses – so if you do forget your lines, the pause will seem natural and once the lines come back you can pick up where you left off without the audience being any the wiser. As Mark Twain said: *'The right word might be effective, but no word was ever as effective . . . [PAUSE] as a pause.'*

In summary, we all feel the fear, we all get nervous. But nerves are good. And you can control them by thinking of Pac-Man – by Practising, Attracting and Chilling. Then, as the adage goes, you can make those *butterflies fly in formation*!

Madam Chairman

14

VARYING THE VOICE I: TURN THAT KNOB!

Mr Chairman, ladies and gentlemen . . . [PAUSE] Let's rerun that a couple of times. [VERY LOUD] Mr Chairman, ladies and gentlemen! Or this: [A WHISPER] Mr Chairman, ladies and gentlemen! Which did you like best? Of course, neither. Too loud and it's uncomfortable for the audience. Too soft and it is irritating – especially if it's a humorous speech and the people in the front row are all creasing up and *you haven't even heard the gag, let alone understood it*!

So how loud should you speak? The answer is simple. Imagine you are having a one-on-one conversation with someone sitting right at the back of the room. Chat to those at the back. Hello, Adam, yes, I'm chatting to you. If you can hear me, so can everyone else. Here's another way of thinking about it. Take your voice and roll it out along the carpet in stages until it gets to the back of the room. Like this: *hello, **hello, HELLO***!

Once you have found your normal speaking volume, next you need to think about varying it. Vocal variety is the very essence of public speaking and the three main ways are through varying volume, pitch and pace. I'll return to the other two in later talks, but this evening let's focus on volume variety.

Suppose I had said earlier: Mr Chairman [NORMAL], ladies [LOUD] and gentlemen [SOFT]. A bit weird, I know, but I hope you get the point. Merely by varying the volume I am giving a different emphasis to the message. I was clearly not interested in talking to the blokes at all. Maybe I was hoping they would ***all clear off and leave me alone with the gals***!

There are times when varying the volume has a specific purpose. If you want to draw the audience in, to make a point that is sensitive or secretive, [SOFT] lower your volume. If yours is a persuasive speech and you want to rouse the audience with a call to arms in your conclusion, [LOUD] *raise the roof*!

But don't be stingy with your volume variety – try varying it throughout a speech or presentation. Variety is the key – in speech as in love. Some disreputable old philosopher, probably me, once said: *the only true aphrodisiac is variety*. So too in public speaking!

Mr Chairman

15

VARYING THE VOICE II: YO YO THAT PITCH!

Madam Chairman, ladies and gentlemen, how many of you here this evening have ever experienced the trials and tribulations of a teenage son? Isn't it a joy?! He comes back from school and you say: 'Hi, lad, how was your day?' [A GRUNT] *'All right.'* 'So what did you do today?' [A GRUNT] *'Stuff.'* You go for something a bit more specific. 'That maths test was today, wasn't it? How did you get on?' [A GRUNT] *'OK.'* And then the phone goes. He rushes over and picks it up: [ANIMATED, HIGH-PITCHED!] *'Hey, Charlie, how you doin', bro?'*

Is this the same person? Are there two species involved here? There are certainly two different voices – one animated, one devoid of any animation at all. One deliberately pitched at the bottom of the barrel, *the other having drunk it*. Pitch is one of the three main ways of conveying variety of voice – along with volume, which we looked at last time, and pace, which we shall look at next time. Vocal pitch is one of the main ways to animate your speech and engage the audience.

What is it about sportsmen and women that makes them so dreary to listen to? Yes, it is that nine out of ten of them deliver their interviews in a monotone. [MONOTONIC SCOTS ACCENT] 'Och, aye, I thought my game came together well in the first two sets. I lost a bit of concentration in the third, but I dug deep, came back in the fourth and closed it out on the tie break'. Contrast that to [ANIMATED NEW YORK ACCENT] *'YOU'VE GOTTA BE KIDDING ME!'*

John McEnroe's commentating pitch is just like his temperament of old on court, always up and down, always full of vitality. Who would the gallery prefer to watch, McEnroe or Murray? Who would an audience prefer to listen to?

Rugby players, coaches, managers and commentators are even worse. They seem to consider it un-cool to vary their pitch. Perhaps it is considered effeminate in that most macho of worlds. They all set a tone as low as that of my teenage son – and stay there. Only one commentator varies his pitch and that is why he is so sought after. Anyone? Yes, Jonathan 'Jiffy' Davies, *as lively a commentator as he was a fly half*. He is the exception who proves the rule.

So, ladies and gentlemen, set yourselves a standard pitch which is at the middle of your range and vary it as you speak. Run it up a bit for variety or even further for something exciting or light-hearted, even a gag. Run it down for more variety or even further for something serious or solemn. It is as simple as that. Run it up, run it down. Avoid the monotone.

Now, just because both my exemplars, McEnroe and Davies, were Celts, don't think that if you're not a Celt you can use that as an excuse. Think of David Attenborough in his documentaries of the natural world – he has wonderful variations of pitch, as well as pace and volume. Or, somewhat less glamorously, Monty Don on *Gardeners' World*, who is one of the most vibrant communicators on television. *And they are both stiff upper lip English!*

So, next time you speak, yo-yo that pitch up and down, up and down. ***Think Andy Parsons – not Jack Dee!***

Madam Chairman

16

VARYING THE VOICE III: PLAY WITH PACE!

Madam Chairman, ladies and gentlemen, let me tell you what I love most in public speaking . . . [LONG PAUSE] That was it – the pause. Yes, it is the simplest and most dramatic way in which you can draw the audience into your speech. It adds that frisson of excitement, that element of tension.

Compare these two introductions: 'Please welcome our keynote speaker for tonight, the luscious Linda Lovelace' and 'Please welcome our keynote speaker for tonight, the luscious . . . [SHORT PAUSE, THEN UP VOLUME AND PITCH] *Linda Lovelace'*. That little pause not only builds the suspense, but encourages you to raise the pitch and exaggerate the crescendo.

Varying the pace of a speech or presentation is the third main tool of vocal variety, along with volume and pitch, which we have discussed in earlier meetings. You can [SPEAK FAST] speed things right up in passages of excitement and [SPEAK SLOW] slow things right down in passages of seriousness. And you can use the pause in both. In either case the pause magnifies the effect – in an exciting passage, it can be the prelude to a punchline and in a serious passage it can help convey the gravity of the situation.

This club was founded twenty-three years ago by an American couple, both highly-experienced speakers, but with diametrically different styles. Lee was tall, slim and elegant, with a fluid, eloquent, articulate, lively, textbook American speaking style. Her husband, Bob, was short, bald and possessed of the kind of paunch sported by middle-aged cowboys in checked shirts and baggy Levis leaning against the fence at the county rodeo and greeting you with *'Howdy, hombre!'* She looked like a TV presenter, *he looked like her chauffeur*.

But when Bob spoke he captivated the audience. He spoke . . . [PAUSE] *liiiiiiike thiiiiiiiis!* He took his time. He was never in a hurry. In a seven-minute speech he got through about one third the number of words of his wife. He made you wait, and wait some more, but when he got there you were seldom disappointed. Now and again he would double or treble his pace – and you were almost *leaping out of your seat in excitement*!

Ladies and gentlemen, play with pace. Speed things up, slow things down, and don't forget the pause. Which reminds me – did you hear the news the other day, about the grizzly bear that escaped from London Zoo? After a few hours it was discovered ambling along Sloane Street. It pushed its way through the front door of the Cadogan Hotel, padded through to the bar and said to the barman: 'Uuuh, aaah, gimme a scotch aaaaaand . . . [LONG PAUSE] soda.' 'Fine,' replied the barman, 'but why the big pause?' 'Uuuh, aaah, I don't know,' replied the bear, *'I was born with them!'*

Madam Chairman

17

MOVING THE BODY I: FREE YOUR FACE!

Mr Chairman, ladies and gentlemen, what would you think if I addressed you like this? [EYES ON FLOOR] Nervous? Shy? Shifty? Guilty? Or what about like this? [EYES UP AT CEILING] *A bit kooky, like Jack Nicholson in* **One Flew Over the Cuckoo's Nest***?*

Do I look like someone who wants to get a message across to the audience? Do I look like I want to communicate?

But what about if I fix you with a good sincere look and talk directly at you, Carol*, for five to ten seconds? Then I move on to someone else and talk to you, sincerely, unthreateningly, for another five to ten seconds. Now I'm communicating. Then I work the room in a Z pattern from back to front, front to back. Is that OK? Am I communicating? I must take care though not to outstay my welcome in the eyes on any one person. *Unless, of course, there is mutual interest, Carol!*

Think too on how to use your eyes or eyebrows as a prop. Default mode should of course be twinkling, complementing the smile on your face. But how about being puzzled? [RAISE EYES TO TOP LEFT] Or surprised? [RAISE EYEBROWS] *Or, for Carol, interested?* [RAISE EYEBROWS TWICE!]

By the way, has anyone here seen traditional Balinese dance? The young girls use their eyes to move the story along. [ADOPT

---

* Note: The very same Carol of Speech 3!

45

STANDARD BALINESE DANCE POSTURE — KNEES BENT, ARMS BENT, HANDS UP, FINGERS BACK — AND FLICK EYES FROM SIDE TO SIDE!] And what about the rest of your face? The mouth is a wonderful prop. The default position should of course be the smile. Mother Teresa said: *'Peace begins with a smile.'* But the mouth is more versatile than that. You can use it to be disapproving [PURSED LIPS]. Or worried [BITE LIPS]. *Or, again, Carol, interested* [LICK LIPS]. If you are very interested indeed, you can try coordinating *eye and mouth movement together* [RAISE EYEBROWS TWICE AND LICK LIPS!]. *Or maybe not!*

Who here is a fan of the TV series *Homeland*? Don't you just worship Claire Danes? She uses her eyes and mouth disturbingly and often weirdly [DEMONSTRATE] in ultra close-ups to convey her inner tensions, frailties and doubts. Try building some of her tricks into your speeches.

Ladies and gentlemen, don't speak with a fixed, rigid, waxwork face. Try playing around with your face, especially your eyes, brows and mouth, to give us variety of expression. That reminds me of an old joke: no offence to Carol, but how do you know when a blonde is about to say something stupid? *She opens her mouth!*

Mr Chairman

18

MOVING THE BODY II: GESTICULA AMICI!

[HANDS IN POCKETS] How presidential do I look today?

Madam Chairman, ladies and gentlemen, hands are very important in public speaking. Let's see them. [HANDS OUT OF POCKETS] In the Lib Dem-UKIP debate before the European elections a while back, Nick Clegg spoke throughout with one hand in his pocket. [ONE HAND IN POCKET] He was trying to look casual, presumably, but – to me – he just looked like a loser.

I coach my son's football team. On a damp, cold winter's day, we gather round for a briefing on the next drill and half of them have their hands in their pockets. Excuse me, lads, this is a sports team. Let's look like sportsmen! Get those hands out! Imagine if they were rowers instead of footballers, with hands in pockets. They would be *pulling the oars with their teeth*!

Actually, there's one place even worse than your pockets for your hands to go. Anyone? Yes, on your face. Worst of all, near your mouth. This is your voice box, your speaker system. It must not be impeded at any cost. Yet how often do we find ourselves at meetings where someone will speak with chin firmly clasped by hands?

Hands need to be out and hanging by your side, where they belong, *ape-like*. That's the default position. But that's not where they stay. That's where they come back to rest after they've been on an excursion. These excursions are called . . . anyone? Yes, gestures. Gestures should be used for a purpose, typically for description, clarification or emphasis.

For example: 'the fish was this big' [ARMS OUT WIDE]; 'the difference between the political parties is tiny' [THUMB AND FOREFINGER ONE CENTIMETRE APART]; *'she emerged from the sea as if from an ocean of dreams!'* [SHAPE AN EXTREME HOUR GLASS].

But don't go over the top, unless it comes naturally to you. The Italians love their gestures: [ITALIAN ACCENT, ARMS WAVING ALL OVER THE PLACE] *'We call-a Roma la citta eterna becos-a eet-a ees-a la casa universale di civilizzazioni.'* Fine, if you're Italiano. *But, if not, you'll just look silly.*

We had a wonderful speaker called Patrick at this club in the 1990s and he used a different hand movement for almost each word that he spoke. [GESTURES FOR EACH ITALICISED WORD!] It was his *own personal style*, *adapted* from his *Ghanaian roots*, and it was *highly effective* and *mesmerising*.

But for [GESTURES AGAIN] *us mortals,* we should use them sparingly and with considered effect. Stay clear of nervous clasping [CLASP], strangling the lectern [GRAB] or hostile accusing [POINT AT AUDIENCE]. But by all means, when you win your next speaking contest, use gestures such as these . . . *[THUMBS UP!]* . . . *[V FOR VICTORY!]* . . . *[POINT AT CHEST!]* . . . *[ROYAL WAVE, WITH SMUG SMILE!].*

Madam Chairman

19

MOVING THE BODY III: ALL THE STAGE IS YOUR WORLD!

[STAND WITH BACK TO WALL] Can you spot anything different about my speaking tonight? Yes, what am I doing over here, back against the wall? What am I running away from? Who's spooking me? Why am I not here in my normal position? [MOVE TO ONE YARD FROM FRONT ROW]

Mr Chairman, ladies and gentlemen, what you do with your body on stage is very important in public speaking. First things first, you need to get into the right place and adopt the right stance. Centre stage and one yard from the front row is where you need to be. And you should place one foot in front of the other. This gives you maximum flexibility to move forward to make a point – and move back when you want to give the audience time to take it in, or take a break before the next point.

Can anyone tell me what the matter is with this position? [LEGS APART] Yes, two main problems. You are rooted to the spot, so it's difficult to move around. And it's overly aggressive. Fine, if you are a gun-slinging cowboy at the OK Corral at a shootout at dawn. Not so fine if you are trying to engage with the audience. And a tad awkward if you are a woman – it sends the wrong signals, **unless your name is Rihanna**. [GRAB IMAGINARY MIKE, GYRATE HIPS!]

Now how about moving around the stage during the speech? There are a few hard and fast rules. Some do, some don't. Think on comedians. Jack Dee stays put. Michael McIntyre paces incessantly from side to side, like he has **ants in his pants**.

Personally, I too like to move around the stage, *but minus the ants*. I am not moving just for the sake of moving, but with a purpose – two of them actually. Loosening up physically helps you relax mentally. And it helps with communicating your message. If you move from one side of the stage to the next [MOVE], it helps gain rapport with the audience, to draw them in – half the audience at a time.

Best of all though is when you move to illustrate or dramatise your message. So if your speech is about doing the triathlon, let's have the full works – swimming [DO CRAWL STROKE], cycling [DO CYCLING ACTION], running [RUN ON THE SPOT]. [PANT HEAVILY] *Now you know why I don't do triathlons!* And if you are speaking about sex, let's have the full works [PREPARE HIP THRUST AGAIN] – *just kidding!* Don't go there – *please leave it to our imagination*!

Ladies and gentlemen, be aware of your body. As Olivia Newton-John once said: [SING] *'Let me hear your body talk'*. Let your body talk on stage. That reminds me of the old joke, when the young man says to his girlfriend: 'Which do you love best, babe, my handsome face or my muscular body?' She takes a good long look at him [EYES UP, DOWN, UP AGAIN] and replies: *'Your sense of humour.'*

Let your body talk. All the world's a stage, said Shakespeare, *but so too is all the stage your world!*

Mr Chairman

20

INTERACTING WITH THE AUDIENCE: GET ENGAGED!

Madam Chairman, ladies and gentlemen, good evening! [PAUSE FOR REPLY] *No, no, no, that's not the right reply!* The correct reply is 'Good evening, Mr President', so let's try that again . . . Good evening, ladies and gentlemen! *Oh dear, oh deary me, what a bunch . . . !*

Now, as you know, that is one of my standard ways of opening a meeting. But why do I do that? Anyone? Yes, because it's one way of warming up the audience, engaging with the audience, right from the off. Does it work?! Well, sorry if it irritates you, *but at least it wakes you up*!

The most common form of audience interaction is to ask questions. It is the device of the teacher, the lecturer. They know that if they don't ask questions the class will fall asleep. Questions keep the students alert and engaged. Here are three common types of question: the hands-up, the Q&A and the loaded. Most common is the hands-up: *Who here likes kissing?* [BLOW KISS!] Don't be shy! Then there's the Q&A: *What makes for a good kiss?* Interesting . . . ! Then there is my favourite, the loaded question: *Who here agrees that lovers kiss better than spouses? Oops!*

Asking questions is the most basic level of interaction. More advanced interaction is when you get the audience to do things which are more active: to stand up, or talk to the person sitting next to them, or write down their thoughts. This can be powerful. We'll try something along those lines in a minute, but first let me give each of you a number, which I hope you'll remember: 1234, 1234 . . .

Now, ladies and gentlemen, as you all know, this year is the 100th anniversary of the start of the Great War*. This is an event which on occasion still overwhelms me with grief. *No, Aldous, I didn't fight in it.* But my grandfather did and he was severely and ultimately mortally wounded in it. What I can never quite come to terms with is the enormity of the catastrophic loss of life – and all for no meaningful purpose whatsoever.

Six years or so ago, I took my son to see the battlefield sites in Flanders and Picardy. Who here has been? I encourage you all to go – they are dignified, humbling and immensely moving. Most poignant of all is the memorial and museum at Beaumont-Hamel in honour of the Royal Newfoundland Regiment. There they have also kept many of the trenches in good condition and you can get a genuine feel for the conditions experienced by the soldiers – especially chilling when I was there as the ground was covered in snow. One thing that takes you aback is that the trenches were so close to each other – less than a hundred paces away – *that's under ten seconds to the likes of Usain and me*!

Now, may I please ask you all to stand up? Thank you very much. At 7.30 a.m. on the first of July 1914, the first day of the Battle of the Somme, the Royal Newfoundland Regiment went over the top of their trenches and charged the enemy lines. Now, would all those of you with the numbers 1, 2 and 3 please sit down. [PAUSE] The Royal Newfoundland Regiment lost 75 per

* This speech was delivered in 2014.

cent of its men that morning. In half an hour. Only one in four was left standing. [PAUSE] Those left standing were not braver, tougher or smarter than those who fell. [PAUSE] They were just luckier. [PROLONGED PAUSE] Please be seated. [PAUSE]

Madam Chairman

TOP TEN DOS AND DON'TS IN DELIVERING THE SPEECH OR PRESENTATION . . . NOT!

- **Do** be afraid – fear endears you to the audience

- **Do** speak without expression – vocal variety is for the stage, not the speech

- **Do** keep your face composed – movement of eyes, brows or mouth is for the clown

- **Do** place your hand on your face, even your mouth, if you wish – it conveys gravitas

- **Do** stand upright, even to attention – a relaxed stance is for the pub

- **Don't** look audience members in the eye – that is rude and intrusive

- **Don't** pause – we'll think you've forgotten your lines

- **Don't** move your hands – that is so Mediterranean

- **Don't** wander around – stick to your spot

- **Don't** interact with the audience – maintain your distance, be aloof

PART IV:
SPEAKING
WITH PURPOSE

21

SPEAKING INFORMATIVELY: GIVE US INFO PLUS!

Madam Chairman, ladies and gentlemen, who here believes that with newspapers, radio, TV, the internet and social networking sites we suffer from information overload? Me too. And yet we still find ourselves having on occasion to give an informational speech. Against all that background noise, it had better be good!

I think the trick is to give a speech that gives the audience not just info, but info plus. An info plus speech has three ingredients: it is on a subject that the audience is interested in, it is well researched and, third, it entertains us at the same time.

The first covers ground I have spoken of before – knowing your audience and choosing a topic that you believe your audience is interested in OR you have strong grounds for believing they could well be interested in. This audience may know little of the proposed EU financial transaction tax and *I suspect you are content to stay that way*! You may also know little of the Zumba fitness craze, but may well be curious to find out more. *After all, J-Lo does Zumba, and, you never know, she may pop in to your class when she's in town!*

Second, the speech needs to be well researched, often from personal experience but, if not, from thorough, usually web-based research. And it should be presented with a well-argued, well-structured supporting case. So you could tell us of how Zumba was created by a Colombian aerobics instructor who forgot his standard dance tapes one day, so he substituted his own tapes of salsa and merengue and found that his class loved it. He took his idea to Miami, licensed the concept to a fitness club and watched it sweep through America and the world. *Zumbanential growth!*

Finally, and most importantly, give us some light relief. Think Robbie Williams: [SING] *Let me entertain you!* Don't give us a seven-minute lecture, full of facts, numbers and percentages. Give us some anecdotes too, of yourself, people you know, people we know of or people who have interesting stories. Let *you* entertain *us* – as well as inform us.

For example, there was this yummy mummy at my local Zumba class in Richmond and she was telling the group that she was having problems getting her tomatoes to ripen. It so happened that the Zumba instructor was a keen gardener and he advised her to try dancing Zumba in front of the tomatoes, at midnight, stark naked, and *the tomatoes would turn red with embarrassment*. The next week at Zumba class she reported back that she had indeed done what she had been advised. She had done some Zumba routines at midnight in the garden, minus her kit, but it hadn't worked. The tomatoes were still green – *but the corn on the cob had grown a couple of inches!*

In summary, ladies and gentlemen, in your informative speeches give us info plus – a topic we would like to hear about, some interesting research and a dash of entertainment too – *even a corny joke! Get it? Corny? Corn on the cob?! Yet another crop failure!*

Madam Chairman

22

SPEAKING ENTERTAININGLY: EVOKE AND EXCITE!

Mr Chairman, ladies and gentlemen, here is a quote that I love: 'I would rather entertain and hope that people learned something than educate people and hope they were entertained.' Who do you think said that? It was Walt Disney. I'm not sure what exactly my kids learned from *The Little Mermaid*, *Aladdin* or *Mulan*, but one thing is for sure: ***they loved those movies almost as much as their dad***!

There is a common misconception that an entertaining speech is the same as a humorous speech. Not so. A humorous speech is indeed an entertaining speech, but there are other kinds of entertaining speeches. Perhaps the most common, and in many ways the easiest for an inexperienced speaker to embark on, is a light-hearted description of pursuing a hobby – perhaps funny in parts, but not necessarily so. Or you could try a dramatic story. Drama can entertain just as much as humour. Think of a TV drama like *Downton Abbey*, not funny, I am told, but, judging by its popularity on both sides of the Atlantic, entertaining.

I shall talk about humorous speaking in another speech, but here are two tips when giving a non-humorous entertaining speech. Make it <u>evocative and exciting</u>. Think on this equation: Evocative + Exciting = Entertaining. First, make it evocative. Paint a picture, transfer the pictures in your mind into ours, with words, gestures, props. If it's your story, place the audience in your shoes. Let us see what you see, hear what you hear, feel the emotions that you feel.

I recall a wonderful speech by Tanya on her maiden venture into skydiving – an activity many of us can relate to even if we would never dream of doing it. She took us through the whole process, step-by-step. She came dressed as if for the jump and strapped on the harness right in front of us. She took us with her through the one-day training session at the airfield, the take-off, the flight itself . . . ! It was alive, vivid, evocative. And tense. It reminded me a bit of an inter-island flight I was on in the Caribbean many years ago, when the pilot of the eight-seater circled the destination island two or three times, clearly looking for a runway, and then this laid-back, Antiguan voice came over the transcom: *'Bear with me here, guys, this is my first time . . . !'*

And make it exciting. Keep us on our toes as the story develops, use plenty of vocal variety, in volume, pace and pitch – raise the pitch when things get really exciting. And end the speech with a bang – perhaps with a humorous twist. Or just follow the natural progression of the story to reach its climax. Tanya couldn't go wrong with her topic, building up the anticipation and fear through the flight, the wait, the door opening, the view of the drop-zone, until . . . *THE JUMP!* [STAR JUMP!]

In summary, ladies and gentlemen, when seeking to entertain us with a narrative or dramatic story, remember Evocative + Exciting = Entertaining. Let me end with a final thought on entertainment, this one from the American comedienne, Lea DeLaria: 'As a stand-up, I try to change the world. As an entertainer, I try to entertain. *And as a lesbian, I try to pick up the prettiest girl in the room.'*

Mr Chairman

23

SPEAKING HUMOROUSLY: PHONE EET!

Mr Chairman, ladies and gentlemen, how scary are these words: 'Stand up, speak – and make us laugh!' Most of us tremble at the thought of the first two commands. But make people laugh as well?

There is no getting round it: humorous speaking is no pushover. Even the funniest speakers have their days when the audience stays shtum. But it is a challenge. It is fun. And if you follow some basic rules you can make a good fist of it. Think on these words of John Cleese: *'Whoever is going to write a script in which a guy like me gets the girl? Me!'*

The first thing to realise is that humorous speaking is not stand-up comedy. Stand-ups earn their bread and butter by performing in front of a boozed-up audience and have no choice but to feed them a gag every other sentence. Humorous speaking is much less demanding. It is about creating a mood, a vibe, a humorous atmosphere surrounding you and your words, one that draws the audience to you. You are seeking not hilarity but conviviality.

Second, the topic. Make it quirky. Think of a quirky situation, a quirky character, a quirky trait. Or think of an ordinary situation and take a quirky slant on it. For example, I heard Jack Dee speak at the Apollo, for ten minutes, on the fact that you only pay a toll going one way on the Severn Bridge. This makes sound economic sense on any bridge toll, but, in his interpretation, you pay to get into Wales, *but not to get out*. That's because, he says, *people drive so fast just to get the hell out of Wales, they would never stop*! I say that people pay to come into Wales . . . [FLICK

BACK IMAGINARY HAIR, JENNIFER ANISTON STYLE] . . . *because we're worth it!*

Better still, take a quirky situation and make it personal. Either tell a story of something quirky that happened to you or invent one. But try to make it self-deprecating. That's why *the French can't do humorous speaking* – but we Brits are brilliant at it, *because we're so rubbish!* At least we were, *until the London Olympics!*

Third, now you have your story, there are three tricks to the trade: Embellish, Extend and Twist. That's EET – like an *elongated version of that little chap who wanted to phone home!* First, embellish – don't tell the story as it happened, exaggerate it. Think Jeremy Clarkson and his *Sunday Times* column – his whole humorous style is based around gross exaggeration. For example, that blonde who cornered you in the alleyway, by the Stage Door, and asked for your autograph? – *she wasn't like this* [HANDS CARVE HOUR-GLASS SHAPE], *she was like this!* [HANDS WAY IN FRONT OF CHEST].

And extend. When you get to a funny point in your speech, hold it there. Milk it. Give the audience more. Give us three laughs instead of one. I gave a speech a few years ago about going for an interview and I walked into the room and found this man with his feet up on his desk, reading the newspaper – true story. He stayed that way for five minutes, completely ignoring me, while I squirmed in my seat. What was I supposed to do, I asked the audience. *Whistle a happy tune?* [WHISTLE] *Powder my nose?* [DAB NOSE] *Punch his?* [PUNCH] I could have left it at 'whistle a happy tune', because the audience was with me, sharing my discomfort at the situation. But I extended twice – and the laughs got bigger each time.

Finally, the twist. Save the best to the last. End with a twist, a surprise, something unexpected.

Ladies and gentlemen, humorous speaking is great fun. Find a quirky topic, personalise it and apply the EET tricks of the trade. Then you too can one day become as humorous . . . *as Piers Morgan! That was the twist!*

Mr Chairman

24

SPEAKING IMPROMPTU: BE 3C, DO 3S!

Madam Chairman, ladies and gentlemen, who here loves impromptu speaking? How many of you leap to your feet when your name is called? Or do you, like me, frequently drag yourself wearily from your chair and eke out the seconds as you walk slowly, very slowly to the stage?

But why? Why the grief? Remember the words of Winston Churchill, he of the razor-sharp repartee on the floor of the house: *'The best impromptu speech takes two weeks to prepare.'* So even if he had to cheat, why should we be so hard on mere mortals like ourselves?! Instead, let us walk head held high on to the stage and be the 3Cs and do the 3Ss. The 3 Cs are simple: keep Cool, Calm and Collected. Just chill. *Hmmnn, that's 4 Cs.* Whatever, don't panic. Chill. And do the 3 Ss: Speechify, Stream and Segue.

First, speechify. An impromptu speech is a speech, if typically rather a short one. That means it should have an opening, body and conclusion. And remember that the most important part of any speech is the conclusion. It is the audience's lasting memory of your speech. Save the best till the last, end with a punch and *all your rambling in the middle may be forgiven, if not forgotten!*

Second, stream. Take care not to head into a dead end or you'll find yourself having to repeat yourself just to spin out time. Open up a second stream. There are two common ways to do that. You could try: 'When I was younger, I used to think that way, etc. etc. . . . ', then move on to: 'Now, many years on, I think this way. . . ' Or you could use the third person: 'In the old days, people thought/behaved/acted . . . ', followed by 'these days, people . . . ' This timeline should help you fill out the speech logically and fluently. Alternatively you could try: 'On the one hand, proponents believe . . . ' and then move on to: 'On the other hand, opponents believe . . . ' That also gives you time to *make up your mind which side of the fence you're going to come down on!*

Finally, segue. If you don't particularly like the topic, try segueing into a topic that you do like to talk about – even better, one you have practised beforehand! But make sure the new topic has at least some relevance to the intended topic – and that you can get back on track before the conclusion. A few years ago I was feeling particularly incensed at the scheduling of international rugby matches on Friday nights to suit the TV viewer as opposed to the long distance travelling supporter. I was given the topic: 'a memorable holiday'. So I started by saying that I had enjoyed some wonderful, lengthy trips to the Caribbean, Fiji and Thailand over the years, but the most memorable of all was a long day trip with my dad from my home town of Aberystwyth to Cardiff in 1967 to see Wales wallop England 34–21 – whereupon I was able to segue onto my favourite whinge. I didn't win best speaker, *but I felt a whole lot better for getting the rant off my chest!*

So, in conclusion, be cool, calm and collected and do the 3Ss – speechify, stream and segue. And soon you'll be able to think on your feet and speak off the cuff like Churchill himself – *with a couple of weeks prep beforehand!*

Madam Chairman

25

STORYTELLING: GET WET!

Madam Chairman, ladies and gentlemen, are you sitting comfortably? Then let me begin. *Once upon a time, in a land far away . . .*

Oh, those were the days, when we used to listen to our mum, dad or granddad, or a teacher, tell us a story. Since then some of us have done the same thing in turn to our kids, our grandkids, *our spouse . . . !*

Despite the advent of radio, TV, PlayStation and the iPod, the joy of storytelling does not abate. As Groucho Marx said: *'If you've heard this story before, don't stop me. I'd like to hear it again.'* But there are good stories and those not so good. Here are three tips on how to tell a good story, to be remembered via a rather esoteric texting acronym. It is a close relation of the better-known LOL. It is WML, *Wetting Myself Laughing!*

First the W, the word pictures. Let's set the scene, the place, the time, the weather, the atmosphere, the ambience, the surroundings. Try and evoke all five senses. So, for example, don't just tell us that Little Red Riding Hood set out into the wood. Tell us how she set forth into *the forest, that dark, damp, musky, creaky, clinging, foreboding, spook-infested forest . . .*

Then there is the M, for meaning. A story may or may not have a moral, but if there is no moral then there still needs to be a meaning. Otherwise how can the audience truly engage? The meaning may be simply to amuse us – in which case it had better be humorous throughout. The audience needs something to take away. Thus, for example, if I told you a story about how I wormed my way backstage at the O2 into Beyoncé's dressing room, I should tell you exactly how I did it. It was easy: ***I went to sleep, woke up and I had done it!***

And finally the L: we need to live the story. It needs to be vivid. We should use the face to show the emotions of the characters, use the hands to demonstrate the action, and above all, use the voice to both caress and entertain the audience. We should use the full range of vocal variety – for example, role playing the dialogue or making background sounds, for example of wind or rain, cars or trucks, cats or dogs.

Best of all we could interact with the audience and get them to make the sounds. Let's try this: just rub the palms of your hands together like this . . . [RUB] That is the sound of drizzle. Now brush your palms up and down like this . . . [BRUSH] That is the sound of light rain. Here's heavy rain . . . [CLAP] And here's hail and thunder . . . [STRIKE CUPPED PALMS ONTO BACK OF THIGHS]. ***We have created an auditory rainstorm!***

In summary, ladies and gentlemen, if you want to tell us a story, remember to get wet, remember WML. Create word pictures, make it meaningful and live the story. And here's a final thought on storytelling from Orson Welles: *'If you want a happy ending, that depends, of course, on where you stop the story!'*

Madam Chairman

26

TELLING A TALL TALE: THINK BIG FISH, THINK COD!

Mr Chairman, ladies and gentlemen, the last time we met I sang one line of one song. One note, the last, was a perfect baritone top E, which penetrated the back wall of this room, through the adjacent meeting room and right into the bar. There it cracked the miniature, delicate, elegant chandelier. A shard of glass fell down and struck an Iranian gentleman on the top of his bald head. All he had been doing until then was work his way harmlessly through a chilled bottle of Dom Pérignon, assisted by his striking blonde companion, dressed in a faux fur coat, fishnet stockings, stiletto heels . . . and, if truth be told, little else. She rushed shrieking to the reception saying that her 'friend' had been the victim of an assassination attempt. The receptionist called the Iranian Embassy, the ambassador called the Ayatollah, the Ayatollah pressed the red button and a missile strike was launched . . . *on Russell Brand!*

It all started right here, in this room, with one note, from one line, of one song, *but what a remarkable ending!*

Ladies and gentlemen, that was a tall tale, not a great one, but, believe me, *I've told worse!* Nevertheless it had all the right constituents of a tall tale speech: it was credible, organised and deadpan. That's C-O-D, cod, *as in the fish that flavours the chips!*

First, the C. The tale needs to be credible, or at least credibly incredible. You might choose a credible character who can do unlikely – even incredible – things, like a superhero. Or you might find yourself in a credible situation or facing a credible problem and resolving it in an unlikely, even incredible, way. Thus it is credible that a musical note can crack glass. It is also credible that the Ayatollah has a red button to hand. *Indeed the whole tale was credible: it happened!*

Second, keep the tale O for organised. Have an opening that sets the scene and describes the character or the situation. Have a body that develops the tale clearly and shows how the situation is resolved. And then end with a bang, preferably humorous and, best of all with a twist. You all thought the Ayatollah would strike on Israel, but, no, *he is smart – he knew that the real threat to global sanity came from a narcissistic and intensely irritating comedian!*

Finally, D for deadpan. You can only carry off a tall tale if you convey the impression that it happened. And that means a straight face. Think Jack Dee. I'm not sure his face is even capable of a smile. Your face must be deadpan throughout. If I had laughed and joked through my Iranian tale, you wouldn't have believed me. *But I didn't – and you did!*

In summary, ladies and gentlemen, for a tall tale speech think credible, organised and deadpan: think C-O-D, think cod – as in *the cod that flew [WAVE ARMS] all the way from the North Sea and crash landed in my suburban garden pond [DO BIG SPLASH]. It was THIS BIG! [ARMS WIDESPREAD]*

Mr Chairman

27

SPEAKING INSPIRATIONALLY: IT S QED!

Mr Chairman, ladies and gentlemen, [IN MARTIN LUTHER KING VOICE] 'I have a dream . . . ', [IN CHURCHILL VOICE] 'we shall fight on the beaches . . . ', [IN ALEX FERGUSON VOICE] *'yer get oot there – and knobble 'em!'* – that was Alex Ferguson, by the way, delivering one of his famous hair dryer talks!

How do you inspire an audience? What are the constituents of an inspirational speech? Actually I looked up the definition of an inspirational speech on a reputable website. It said thus: 'An inspirational speech is one that truly inspires the audience.' *Very helpful*. Nevertheless, there are three key elements of speaking inspirationally: establish your Qualifications, involve the Emotions of your audience and use the Ditto. *That's QED!*

Ferguson didn't need to establish his qualifications, his credentials, his authority – his select audience knew exactly who he was. They knew he had a mansion full of silverware. But we do. So when we give an inspirational speech we need to set out why our opinion matters. I coach my son's junior football team and when I give them a rousing talk before the match I may need to remind them that I am a former international – *for the British Virgin Islands*. True – when I used to live there in the 1970s, we once played a team from a *visiting Royal Navy warship. I came on as a sub – in the last three minutes*!

Second, inspiration is all about emotion, not fact. An inspirational speech speaks to the heart, not the head. Let me give you one example, quite appropriate close to the centenary of the outbreak of the Great War. In April 1917, the USA finally declared war on Germany, fighting alongside the British, rather than against them, for the first time since independence, 141 years earlier. The British Prime Minister, David Lloyd George, gave an address to the US Ambassador in London and he used emotion to inspire the American people in the worthiness of their decision. Here is an extract:

I rejoice as a democrat that the advent of the United States into this war gives the final stamp and seal to the character of the conflict as a struggle against military autocracy throughout the world.

The United States of America have the noble tradition, never broken, of having never engaged in war except for liberty. And this is the greatest struggle for liberty that they have ever embarked upon.

The third factor, the D in QED, is the ditto, the repetition. In his address Lloyd George uses the words 'free', 'freedom' or 'liberty' twenty-five times. He praises the American people for having fought for their own freedom and for having inspired the subsequent revolutions in France and Russia. Through this conflict, they could do the same for Germany. Here's another extract:

When France in the eighteenth century sent her soldiers to America to fight for the freedom and independence of that land, France also was an autocracy. But Frenchmen in America, once they were there – their aim was freedom, their atmosphere was freedom, their inspiration was freedom. They acquired a taste for freedom, and they took it home. And France became free.

So, ladies and gentlemen, should you wish to give an inspirational speech, remember it's not hard. It's quite easily done, QED. Establish your qualifications, speak to the emotions and hammer the message home through ***the power, the great power, the inspirational power – of the ditto.***

Mr Chairman

28

MOTIVATING THE TEAM: SHOW THE CAP FITS

Madam Chairman, ladies and gentlemen, I talked the other day about the constituents of an inspirational speech. This evening I would like to talk about a close relative, the motivational speech, typically delivered to a team – of employees or sports players or fellow society members.

Here are three tips on delivering a motivational talk: think C for culture, A for ardour and P for progress – that's C-A-P, or cap. As Bob Marley once philosophised: [SING] *'Who the cap fit, let them wear it!'*

First, remind them of the culture. The most successful organisations, according to Professor Jim Collins, have an almost cult-like culture, with a common ideology and common purpose. This club, for example, rightly prides itself on its sense of fun, its bonhomie, its buzz. Mahatma Gandhi said that *'Culture resides in the hearts and the soul of the people'*.

Which brings me to the second tip, the ardour – the spirit, the passion. A motivational speech must rouse the emotions, the feelings. We often hear how the motives for terrible crimes are those of fear, passion, envy, jealousy, greed, revenge. But such powerful emotional intensity can be channelled into a positive, beneficial force. Oprah Winfrey said: *'Passion is energy. Feel the power that comes from what excites you.'*

The final part of the CAP is the P, the progress. It is not enough to appeal to the culture and to rouse the ardour, you have to engage the mind too. And the way to do this is by highlighting signs of progress – real, definitive, incontrovertible signs of progress, no matter how small. Show momentum. This will help the team believe that they are making positive, discernible steps towards the goal they seek.

I could end with an example about how Steve Jobs motivated the Apple team, or how José Mourinho elevates each team he manages to a new level, but instead let me end with a personal example. My son's football team, which I manage, got walloped by their closest rivals 7–3 one Sunday. By a quirk of the fixture list we found ourselves playing these same opponents again the following Sunday. In my team talk before the game, I applied the CAP approach to the letter. I reminded them of our culture – originating from a bunch of eleven-year-old schoolmates kicking the ball around in the park just for fun on a Saturday morning. I appealed to their ardour, in particular their thirst for revenge! And I showed them signs of progress – how in midweek training we had worked on a new formation to stifle the attacking threat of our opponents. It worked like a dream – by half time we were 3–0 up. *Our opponents looked as shell-shocked as the Brazilians did at their World Cup semi-final.*

Ladies and gentlemen, if you embark on a motivational speech, show your team that the CAP fits – remind them of your culture, evoke their ardour and show signs of progress. Let me end by returning to that extraordinary World Cup match, following which the internet was flooded with so many gags that *I couldn't take it a Neymar!* But the one I liked best was a photo of the magnificent 100ft high Christ the Redeemer statue atop Mount Corcovado [STAND WITH ARMS OUTSTRETCHED], overlooking Rio, with the caption: *'We lost by this much!'*

Madam Chairman

29

SPEAKING PERSUASIVELY: BED THE AUDIENCE!

Mr Chairman, ladies and gentlemen, who here has ever been involved, either as the doer or the doee, in the act . . . *of seduction?!*

Don't be shy! Seduction is an important art, a manifestation, if perhaps extreme, of the art of persuasion. In the words of the eighteenth-century writer/philosopher Voltaire: [FRENCH ACCENT] *'Eet ees not enough to persuade, one must learn to seduce'!* So here are three tips on persuasive speaking, taken from the art of seduction: you need to be Believable, Emotive and Demanding. Strangely enough, that happens to spell the acronym *B-E-D!*

First, believable – you and your storyline have to be credible. You need to have both the facts that support your case and the experience that gives your interpretation of the facts credibility. In seduction, the essential fact you need to convey to your audience, typically of one, is that he or she is particularly pleasing to the eye – and in this matter, given your wealth of experience, you can claim to be a *veritable authority!*

Second, emotive. You cannot expect the audience to follow you unless you appeal not just to their head, but to their heart. If your speech is on recycling plastics, don't just rattle off statistics of the tons of plastics which end up floating in the Pacific. Tell us of the scores of albatrosses that die miserably of starvation with their stomachs bloated with plastic. In the art of seduction, the eighteenth-century Venetian philanderer Giacomo Casanova speaks *not of lust, but lurve*. He speaks *not from the loins, but the heart*. He doesn't say [ITALIAN ACCENT] *'ti desidero'*, he says [ITALIAN ACCENT] *'ti amo, mia bellissima.'*

Third, demanding. You must conclude your persuasive speech with a demand, a rousing call to action. Whatever it is you are espousing, be it recycling your waste, voting for UKIP or both – *aren't they the same thing?* – you must conclude with a call to do something about it. In seduction, the process can only conclude with *a coruscating crescendo and a calamitous, cacophonous, cymbal-clashing climax!*

So, ladies and gentlemen, in a persuasive speech just remember these three things: be Believable, Emotive and Demanding. B, E, D. *Your aim is to BED the audience*. I end with some words of wisdom on this theme by the sensual Swiss siren, Ursula Andress, who said: *'I don't use my body to seduce, no. I just stand there!'*

Mr Chairman

30

GIVING FEEDBACK: MANAGE IN THE EPL!

Madam Chairman, ladies and gentlemen. [PICK ON ONE MEMBER OF THE AUDIENCE, ADOPT STERN VOICE] 'Thank you very much for your report, Max, but, to be frank, there is, shall we say, room for improvement. You handed it in a day late, there was no logical flow leading up to your conclusion and your grammar was often AWOL. In short, I expect better next time.'

Who here has ever received feedback like that from a boss? Or even more damning? Who here has ever delivered feedback like that? *Tut, tut!*

Here are three things to remember about giving feedback: Encourage, Praise and Limit. That's EPL, as in the English Premier League. Imagine yourself as a Premier League manager giving feedback to a player after a match.

What is the purpose of such feedback? Yes, it is to encourage the player to do better next time, to improve performance. If your feedback comes in the form of unmitigated criticism, will the player perform better next match? Think rather of a hen and how she encourages her chicks: *she eggs them on!*

Second, your feedback should be in the form of a speech, with an opening, body and conclusion, and both the opening and the conclusion containing solely positive, upbeat messages – in other words, praise. Think on feeding them with a praise sandwich, namely praise/suggest/praise. Praise them for what they have done well, suggest what they could do better, then praise them again for something else they did well. That way they will leave with a spring in the step. Praise, suggest, praise. That's PSP, easily remembered, at least by my son, as ***PlayStation Portable!***

Finally, and good luck with navigating these acronyms, the third rule in giving feedback, the L of the EPL, is to limit the number of suggestions. In that crucial sandwich filler, the S of the PSP, do not give a whole laundry list of suggestions, from A to Z. Limit it to three, maximum. That way they might remember at least one of them.

Here's an example. Who here saw my speech in the tall tale contest a few weeks ago [SEE BOX BELOW]? I thought it was a cracker, ***though the judges clearly didn't!*** Let's do a one-minute evaluation of it . . . [HIGH-PITCHED, POSH VOICE] 'The third speaker was Vaughan Evans, with a speech about his former mistress, named Mata, who could read his mind. The speech was credibly incredible, as with all good tall tales, and it was delivered in Vaughan's usual lively, animated manner. I have two recommendations: Vaughan should take greater care to know his audience, and especially the judges, one or two of whom might have found his material ***somewhat bloke-ish***. And second, one or two of the gags fell a bit flat. I don't know if Vaughan tried them out on anyone before he gave the speech, but that approach usually pays dividends. But it was a rollicking speech, he kept us guessing where he was taking us and he brought the tale to a memorable conclusion with a terrific pun in his punchline. Mr Chairman.'

Now let's evaluate the evaluation, via the English Premier League guidelines. Was it encouraging? Yes, the conclusion was upbeat. Was there a praise sandwich? Yes, it was well balanced. Did it limit the number of recommendations? Yes, just the two

– hence easier to remember and more likely to be put into effect. *Well, we'll see about that . . . !*

Madam Chairman

MINDFUL

Mr Chairman, ladies and gentlemen, I'd like to speak to you tonight about my mistress. Or, to be more precise, I'm sad to say, my former mistress. Mata is as exotic as her name, beautiful, sensual and *. . . never, ever, moody!* Between you and me, I had to add in that last bit, because she could read my mind, literally, every corner of it – and, for all I know, she still can!

This was, of course, a great advantage when first we met. She knew exactly what was on my mind, *so we didn't have to waste time in conversation!* Over the subsequent months, though, that talent of hers became quite difficult to live with.

I remember in particular when we went on a naughty weekend to Barcelona. There we were, strolling down Las Ramblas, when a tall, scantily dressed, dark blonde Catalan beauty rollerbladed by. I did my very best to wrench my eyes away, but, as too often, just a fraction too late. 'You fancy that woman, don't you?' she said. I had tried every excuse over the months but what was the point? She knew, she knew I knew she knew, so I said it: *'Phwoar!' The weekend wasn't a success.*

Then in 2008 came the financial crisis and times became tough for my business. It became evident that I would find it increasingly difficult to keep Mata in the style to which she had become accustomed – the mews cottage in Chelsea, the silver Mini Cooper, *the credit account at Ann Summers.* So we set about thinking how we could monetise Mata's extraordinary talent. The obvious candidate was the TV quiz show, *Who Wants to Be a Millionaire?*

So off we went to Elstree Studios in Borehamwood and I sat in the back row of the auditorium with my iPad. At each question, I Googled, kept my eyes down and my mouth shut. And she read my mind. She zoomed through the early rounds and in no time at all came to the final round. The question was this: is a Zari a variety of A. Apple, B. Banana, C. Chilli or D. Date? I Googled and found out immediately that it was a type of apple. Mata read my mind and answered A. The quizmaster, Chris Tarrant, asked her if that was her final answer, meanwhile thinking that if Mata got the answer right he would have a good excuse to invite this ravishing new millionairess out on a celebratory date. Mata got confused. My mind was pressing for an apple, Tarrant's for a date. She figured I must have got it wrong. *She went for D for date.*

Mata lost her £1 million. Tarrant lost the date. *And I lost my mistress.*

But at least I regained control over my mind. One might almost say, ladies and gentlemen, that it was *mind over Mata.*

Mr Chairman

31

INTRODUCING A SPEAKER: BIG UP, BUILD UP, WARM DOWN!

Mr Chairman, ladies and gentlemen, I went to a university reunion the other day. The chairman stood up and said: 'Hi, everyone, and welcome back to school! We have a packed programme ahead of us this morning so, without further ado, I would like to bring on our first speaker, who of course needs no introduction. Over to you, Tony . . . '

This chairman was a lovely chap and meant well, but he broke just about every rule of introducing a speaker, other than one – he was wearing a big smile. He told us nothing about the speaker, assuming we all knew his background – most did, some didn't; he gave no build-up to the speaker; and later, after the speaker had sat down, moved straight on to a similar non-introduction to the next speaker. So here are three tips for introducing a speaker: big up, build up and warm down.

First, the bigging up. Let's have the background. We don't want a full bio, but we do need to know why this person has earned the right to be talking to us today. Give us a minute or so on why he or she is rather special and has a voice to be reckoned with on the topic in question. Best of all, build in a gag, perhaps around a theme which you have introduced for the day and discussed with the speakers beforehand. Here's an example from an imaginary reunion: 'Our speaker today, ladies and gentlemen, has been in the movie business since the advent of talkies, he is recognised as possessing the quickest wit in Hollywood history and when I asked him if he was proud to be an alumnus of this school, he remarked that *he refused to join any club that would accept him as a member . . .* '

Then the build-up. Don't let your introduction fizzle out, build up the anticipation. After the brief background and preferably the gag, end with a rousing crescendo, of both volume and pitch. Make the audience anticipate with relish the prospect of this person arriving on stage. Thus, in the last example: 'Ladies and gentlemen, please welcome . . . [HIGH PITCH AT END] *Mr Groucho Marx!*'

Finally the warm down. This is too often overlooked by chairmen. And there is no excuse for it. You have the whole length of the speech to think up just the one line, a warm, appreciative, preferably witty line to say as the speaker heads back to his seat. Surely we can all do that?! So, as Groucho takes his seat, the chairman could say: 'Thank you, Groucho, for those quirky memories of schooldays. I guess you are the living proof of one of your more memorable lines: A man is only as old as the woman he feels!'

Ladies and gentlemen, do take trouble with your introductions. Your speakers deserve that at the very least. *Big 'em up, build 'em up and warm 'em down!*

Mr Chairman

32

CONVERSING ONE-TO-ONE: SHUT UP!

Madam Chairman, ladies and gentlemen, were you aware that the very skills you have been learning as a public speaker can hold you in good stead as a conversationalist? And by that I do not mean for you to be like George Bernard Shaw, who said: *'I often quote myself. It adds spice to a conversation.'*

There are two public speaking skills that are especially important in conversing – and there is one other where you have to take special care NOT to apply it in a conversation.

The first skill that is directly transferable concerns the voice. The aim of a conversation, whether at home or in the office, in the pub or at an event, is to keep the other person informed or entertained to such an extent that he or she has no desire to move on from you to the next person. Your content must be good, of course, but so too its delivery. You should remember all you have learnt about variation of vocal tone, volume and pitch. In short, think vocal vitality. Don't overdo it though, like Nancy Astor, who said: *'My vitality repels me. I am the kind of woman I would run from.'*

For the second skill, I need a prop, of the human kind. Thank you, Nicola. Please stand just here and face me. One thing we learn in public speaking is the use of space. We don't stand too far away from the audience, nor at the back of the room. But nor do we stand too close. So too in conversing. An individual has four types of personal space. Nicola's personal space is a circle of 4 feet radius from her. Conversing with her inside this space is a no-no. Her social space is a radius 4 to 12 feet from her. This is where you should be. Her public space is a radius 12 to 25 feet and this is where she would feel comfortable in her public speaking.

There is a fourth and final type of personal space, called the intimate space, which is a circle of radius 1.5 feet from her. That is here! It is where I would be happy to dwell for a while, ***but it is by invitation only!***

We have talked about voice and space. But there is one public speaking skill which we develop that we must not use in conversation – and that is banging on for five to seven minutes without giving the other person a chance to get a word in. And there are, I am afraid, many to be found in speaking clubs who fall into that trap. Truman Capote said: *'A conversation is a dialogue, not a monologue. That is why there are so few good conversations.'* To rectify this, do a quick check after every conversation. What share of voice did I have in that conversation? 50/50, 60/40, 40/60? That's fine. 70/30? I hope I was being especially informative and/or entertaining. 80/20 or more? Was I a bore? *Again?*

So, ladies and gentlemen, improve your conversational skills by deploying those of public speaking. Bring vitality to your voice, be aware of personal space and maintain a balanced share of voice. With regard to the latter point, little has changed since the days of Marcus Tullius Cicero, who wrote: *'Silence is one of the great arts of conversation.'*

Madam Chairman

33

SPEAKING AS BEST MAN: BE BAD!

'Mr Toastmaster, the bride and groom, ladies and gentlemen, it is my great honour to be speaking to you this afternoon as Best Man. I have known Nick for fifteen years and he is a brave man. There is no corner of his past that I do not know about. If there's anyone here who now feels a bit apprehensive or anxious about what lies ahead . . . *it's because you have just married Nick!* Actually I was a bit nervous about speaking today, but Nick told me not to worry. Public speaking is a bit like walking through a nudist camp – *it's only hard for the first minute!*'

Mr Chairman, ladies and gentlemen, that's rule No. 1 in a Best Man speech – start from the off with a gag or two, preferably quite mild. And misleading – because from then on you are going to raise the temperature! So here are my three tips: venture near the bone, develop the anecdotes and don't drink. That's B for bone, A for anecdotes and D for don't drink – in other words, *be BAD!*

Against all sensible advice about taking care not to upset the bride or her parents, let alone maiden Aunt Joan, go for it – all the other wedding speeches should be 'nice', but the best man's job is to induce the odd squirm. Indeed you can take the audience right to the edge, but then rescue them at the last moment. In a best man speech I gave many moons ago, I told the audience of the Stag Weekend I had organised for the groom in Barcelona. I told them how Nick had had a few beers too many, how we had ended up in an insalubrious establishment and how my lasting memory of the night was of the groom getting up close and personal with someone of cool, pale, painted complexion. Her name was *Señorita Armitage Shanks!*

The second tip concerns the anecdotes. Don't stuff your speech with one-liners, pulled from the Web. The delivery of these lines is best left to stand-ups, who these days are all over the telly. Even if you manage to remember all the gags, can you really compete in delivery and timing with the likes of Milton Jones? No, dig up a select few genuine anecdotes about the groom and build them into fully-fledged stories. Then apply the standard humorous speech tricks* of extending, embellishing and twisting. Only then, by all means, build a handful of sure-fire one-liners into the speech, like: 'I can now reveal that the bride and groom are to honeymoon in Wales. *Nick told me that he was going to Bangor for the whole week!*'

Finally, as in any after-dinner speech, don't drink! Not a drop. Nearly everyone else will be merry, with critical capabilities partially suspended. You must be sharp and in control. You will have a ten-minute or so slot. Stay off the booze and you'll keep to it.

In summary, gentlemen, if you have a best man speech on the horizon, be BAD – strike near the bone, develop the anecdotes into stories and don't drink. And how about concluding with something philosophical, like: 'Marriage will do wondrous things for Nick – it will teach him responsibility, loyalty and trust, *all the things he wouldn't have needed if he had stayed single!*'

By the way, as an afterthought, if you're the Best Man, *how come it's not you who is marrying the bride?*

Mr Chairman

---

* Speech 23.

TOP TEN DOS AND DON'TS IN TAILORING THE SPEECH . . . NOT!

- **Do** always speak impromptu – few speeches need preparation

- **Do** stick to the story in storytelling – creating imagery slows the pace

- **Do** stick to reason in an inspirational speech – leave emotion to the Celts

- **Do** have your say in a conversation – speak for at least twice as long as the other person

- **Do** be nice as best man – think only of what the groom's gran would like to hear

- **Don't** excite in an entertaining speech – respect the heartbeat of senior listeners

- **Don't** embellish in a humorous speech – is your name Clarkson?

- **Don't** try to seduce in a persuasive speech – that's just creepy

- **Don't** praise when giving feedback – only fools fall for flattery

- **Don't** waste time when introducing a speaker – name and position are all we need

PART V:
PRESENTING

34

FOCUSING THE CONTENT: SAIL THE 7CS!

Madam Chairman, ladies and gentlemen, who here finds presenting at work nerve-racking? Now keep your hands up if you find presenting *more* nerve-racking than speaking on a general topic to a room or hall full of people? Not one of you!

Yes, presenting at work is a doddle compared to the more public form of public speaking. For two main reasons: the standard of presenting at work is in general abysmal, so expectations tend to be low. And in presenting the use of notes or speaking aids is widely accepted, so you don't have to worry about remembering your lines.

But that doesn't mean that you can waltz into a presentation and carry it off without due care and preparation. You need to focus your content on the needs of your audience, use speaking aids effectively and deliver your presentation clearly. Today I'll talk about the first of these: focusing the presentation.

Let's start at the very beginning. What was the first tip I spoke of in public speaking many months ago? Yes, it was 'know your audience'.* Who are you presenting to? Colleagues, clients, suppliers, partners, financiers? How well do you know them? What tickles their fancy? Should you keep your presentation dead serious or sprinkle it with anecdotes, even humour? What will they wear – will they be in City suits or post-dot com smart

* See Speech 2

casuals? Then remember the old maxim: be as well dressed as the best person in the room!

If you are pitching to financiers, will you be addressing investors or bankers – or both? If the former, accentuate the upside. If the latter, go easy on the upside – they really aren't interested. Point out the downsides, but show them how you will dodge the risks or mitigate them. By the way my wife went to see her banker the other day to ask for advice on how to start a small business. The banker told her: *'Start a large business and bank with us!'*

Presentations to colleagues are usually about providing answers. You are presenting to colleagues the results of an assignment, some research, a study, a plan, a way forward, a status update. They will want to know your take on the matter, your answer to the main question under discussion. It is so too in a pitch to clients, partners or financiers. They expect answers to key questions such as: why should we do business with you, why should we ally with you, why should we back you?

You need to focus your content around delivering that answer, clearly, crisply, concisely, consistently, coherently, credibly and convincingly. You need to sail the 7Cs.

And here's how to do it. Start by giving them the answer to the main question under discussion. Then give them the answers to each of the supporting questions which need to be answered to answer the main question. And so on. In each case, tell them what you are going to tell them. Tell them. Then tell them what you have told them.

For example, take a pitch to a new client. Don't open with ten minutes on the history of your business and how your founder is now retired and working on his handicap down at Valderrama. This is appendix material. Get straight in with the answer. Your client needs your firm as a supplier or partner for these three reasons: A, B and C. Tell them of your qualifications, experience and testimonials for A. Remind them of all three reasons. Tell them your credentials for B. Remind them again of all the reasons. Now tell them your credentials for C. Conclude by reminding them one final time of all three reasons – and sit down.

The message is clear, crisp and concise. It is consistent, even repetitive, but that doesn't matter – reinforcing the message helps ram it home. It is coherent, because it shows that in the areas where the client needs help you are best placed to help them. It is credible, because you have backed up your assertions with fact. Above all, it will be convincing.

Ladies and gentlemen, in summary, focus your content on your audience and sail the 7Cs. Hold on, before I sit down, have I not broken one of my golden rules and failed to inject any light relief into this speech, ***other than a sad gag about a banker?*** That is understandable on this occasion. Sailing the seven seas is a sensitive issue for my family, for I hail from several generations of merchant seamen – ***true!*** My great grandfather was captain of a three-masted clipper and he returned from one voyage to the South Seas with a peg leg and a hook [SHOW CURLED MIDDLE FINGER]. He paid a lot for them – ***an arm and a leg!***

Madam Chairman

35

USING POWERPOINT: USE, DON T ABUSE!

Mr Chairman, ladies and gentlemen, PowerPoint gets a bad press. There, I've said it. I am on the verge of defending the monopolistic megalith that is Microsoft. Did you know, by the way, that Microsoft has recently broken Volkswagen's world record? *VW only ever made 22 million bugs!*

PowerPoint is much ridiculed, not least by Scott Adams's cartoon character, Dilbert. One such cartoon has him asking the presenter if his presentation was intended to be incomprehensible. The presenter ignores him and asks if there are any questions on the content. Dilbert retorts: *'There was content?'*

But in truth, I like PowerPoint. It gets lampooned not because of what it is and what it can do but what people do with it. Business folk misuse PowerPoint to a criminal degree.

It all stems from a misunderstanding of what it is for. Are you using PowerPoint as a visual *aide memoire* to your oral presentation – or as a document of record? Or both?

If you are using PowerPoint as an *aide memoire*, remember these biblical words, from Ecclesiastes, chapter 6, verse 11: 'the more the words, the less the meaning'. Or the later adage that 'a picture is worth a thousand words', updated recently by that great twenty-first century American sage, George W. Bush, who said: *'One of the great things about books is sometimes there are fantastic pictures.'*

PowerPoint cries out for you to use pictures. The scope is unlimited, but too often we fail to take the time to find a good picture or design a chart. Words are easier. But pictures convey the message instantly and more vividly and they remain in the brain for longer – they are what your audience is more likely to take home with them. If you must use words in a pure *aide memoire* PowerPoint presentation, follow these simple rules: no more than a title plus three, max four bullets per slide, and no more than three, max four words per bullet. On average, fifteen to twenty words per slide.

It is when PowerPoint gets used as a document of record that the trouble starts. The worst culprits are the big accounting houses which use PowerPoint in their due diligence reports, blanketing slides with multiple charts and minuscule text in an endeavour to cram as much info as possible into one slide. This is sacrilege – it is just writing a report in landscape form, but less intelligibly.

I confess that, as a consultant in business strategy, I too produce my documents of record in PowerPoint, but I have three techniques to combine the two purposes. First, I use charts, tables and images wherever possible, and animation sparingly. Second, I shove most of the data and wordy stuff into an appendix. Third, I tell a story. I summarise all that is on each slide in a one- or two-line headline at the top of the page, presented in blue, bold, large font. Supporting main points in the body of the slide are also presented in large font bullets, but in black and unbold, with supplementary material indented in smaller point. Thus the slide can be talked over by just picking up on the headline, or the headline along with a bullet or two – but not the sub-bullets, which are there just for the record.

Ladies and gentlemen, use, don't abuse PowerPoint. Use it creatively as a visual *aide memoire*. Or use it as presentation-cum-document-of-record if you must, but with a definitive storyline and a weighty appendix. One final point. Who can see the flaw in Dilbert's chutzpah: *'As I am sure you can clearly see in slide 297 . . . !'*

Mr Chairman

36

DELIVERING THE MESSAGE: RECALL VHS!

Madam Chairman, ladies and gentlemen, who here has ever been to a meeting of colleagues or clients where the presenter's delivery was so abysmal you lost the desire to listen? I went to one such the other day. I learnt a lot. **_Did you know you can bend a paper clip to make a perfect S?_** [START DEMONSTRATION, THEN TOSS IT AWAY!]

There is nothing special or esoteric about presenting. It's just one form, one subset of public speaking. And the rules and guidelines for public speaking apply just the same to presenting. Like structuring your presentation coherently and delivering it clearly. We talked about the former in an earlier speech*, so let's now look at delivery.

There are three aspects of speaking delivery which are most pertinent to presentations. And in so many meetings these aspects go wrong. Fix these and you will be a presenter out of the common. They are: the Voice, the Hands and the Speaking aids – or VHS. Imagine someone is filming your presentation with an old tech VHS video camera. Talking of videos, Joan Rivers had the right idea: **_'I prefer to be in a video, not play with one.'_** And in homage to her recent passing, how about this gem: **_'Comedy needs me! I plan to be around for the next hundred years. Just like herpes!'_**

---

* Speech 34

First, the voice. For whatever reason, too many presenters get the voice wrong. Some feel they should be as casual or laid-back as possible, so their delivery becomes almost soporific. Others think that because everyone is seated around the same table they don't have to speak up. The rule of thumb is the same as in public speaking: you should imagine yourself conversing with the person farthest from you. And animatedly. Imagine that person is your best mate, *or your intended date!*

Second, the hands. This is my personal bugbear. Someone round the table is saying something important resting his forehead in his hand – and it is usually a 'he'! This immediately robs all vitality from the voice. Worse, he is speaking with his chin resting on his hand. This cuts off the main mode of communication entirely. What is it with these guys? Why bother to speak at all if they're going to block the sound-waves from reaching the ears of the audience? If you do nothing else in presenting, please keep your hands off your face! I have found myself on occasion interrupting such guys, saying [HAND UNDER CHIN, PUSHING JAW CLOSED, SO THE WORDS ARE ALMOST UNINTELLIGIBLE!]: *'Shorry, could you wepeat that, pease?!' I haven't yet tried that with a client, though!*

Finally, the S of VHS, the speaking aids. I gave a separate talk on this a few months ago,* but bear in mind most of all the three Rs. Whatever speaking aid you use at your presentation, whether it is notes, a flipchart or, very often, PowerPoint, remember to Read, Reset and Release! Read the note, reset your eyes on the

---

* Speech 5

audience, then, and only then, release the information. Do not look at your notes or laptop while actually speaking. Worst of all, don't speak while looking at the screen, with your back turned to the audience. That may work in the movies, when Marilyn Monroe turns her back on her man and tearfully confesses her love for another, but, unlike us, *she has an unseen boom microphone dangling over her head!*

So, ladies and gentlemen, when delivering your presentation, be aware how you use your VHS – your voice, your hands and your speaking aids. To end, here's one extra tip to get your presentation up and running: don't start with the wimpy 'Unaccustomed as I am . . .' Be bold and plunge straight in with: 'Accustomed as I am to speaking in public, having done so frequently in front of the Prince of Wales, the Duke of Cambridge, *the Black Horse . . . , the Red Lion . . . !'*

Madam Chairman

TOP TEN DOS AND DON'TS IN PRESENTING . . . NOT!

- **Do** fill the PowerPoint slide – we like to see everything at once

- **Do** look at the screen while speaking – be at one with us

- **Do** speak softly – it's rude to raise your voice

- **Don't** be clear – make us work hard to follow you

- **Don't** be crisp – allow us to appreciate the minute details of your work

- **Don't** be concise – what's the rush?

- **Don't** be consistent – life is never that straightforward

- **Don't** be coherent – logic is overrated, we prefer intuition

- **Don't** be credible – no need to show us your evidence, we can do that for ourselves

- **Don't** be convincing – let us make our own minds up

CONCLUSION

37

SPEAKING WITH PASSION: LET IT ZIP!

Mr Chairman, ladies and gentlemen, the first speech I gave as President of this club twelve months ago* revealed the three ultimate secrets of public speaking. Who here can remember them?

Yes, they were 1) structure the speech or presentation with an opening, body and conclusion, 2) look the audience right in the eye and 3) speak with passion. The third secret was voted the most important, so let me give you some tips on how to do just that, how to speak with passion. I have three tips, easily remembered through the acronym: *Z-I-P, zip!*

Let's start at the back for a change: P is for personal. Whether your speech is about you, or an issue you feel passionate about, bring plenty of you into the speech. The more of you in it, the more emotional and resonant it will be. There can be no doubt that the most memorable speech in this club over the last year was Margaret's haunting speech about the Nazi occupation of Poland. But it was not just the horrors of the story that touched

---

* Speech 1.

us, but the way Margaret personalised it, by telling us that this awful story was the first time her father had ever spoken to her about the war. And the last.

The next tip is the I – for inspirational. The more you try and inspire the audience in some way, the more likely you are to inject passion into your delivery. Think back on Keiran's speech the other day about how proud he was to be in the police force, to work in the company of colleagues who regularly put their bodies on the line for the security of each and every one of us citizens. It made me think about if only I could be as passionate about my own profession . . . *of management consulting!* It could have been worse, I suppose. I once put myself forward as a parliamentary candidate. *The electorate knew better.*

And finally, the third tip: the Z is for zing. If you want to speak with passion, *stick some zing into your speech, some oomph, some pizzazz!* Whatever your normal speaking style, accentuate it, exaggerate it – double, treble, quintuple it! Think back to Nela's wonderful tale about falling off a bicycle and not making it to some rave in a neighbouring Czech village. It was full of props, vocal variety and body movement, with her helmet, her pedalling and her breathlessness. *It was full of zing!*

In summary, ladies and gentlemen, the ultimate secret of public speaking is to speak with passion, as much for your speeches as in a TED talk. Make your speech Z for zingy, I for inspirational and P for personal. In short, *let it ziiiiiiiiiiiiiiiiiiip!*

Mr Chairman

POSTSCRIPT

A SAMPLE EVALUATION
OF THESE THIRTY SEVEN SPEECHES!

THE OPENING

Mr Chairman, ladies and gentlemen, and especially Joe*, what a whacky idea! Thirty-seven mini-speeches stuck in a book aiming to teach the reader about speech structure, content and delivery. And, you know what? It works! It does what it says on the cover. It shows us how to survive as a speaker or presenter, and ultimately to shine. Talking of shining, that reminds me of one of my all-time favourite songs from the 1960s cult musical, *Hair*: [SING] 'Let the sun shine . . .' Joe's book is indeed a ray of sunshine, it lets the sun shine in to where, for many tentative speakers, [AMERICAN ACCENT] *the sun don't shine!*

THE BODY: PRAISE

There are three things I liked in particular about Joe's book: the structuring, the speaking tips and the light relief.

Joe adopts a very simple speech structure – an opening, body and conclusion and with the body typically consisting of three points. This is a standard speech structure. It is not the only one,

---

* Note: In the interests of avoiding excess schizophrenia, the author of this book is taken in this evaluation to be one Joseph Bloggs!

but it is the simplest and very often the most effective, whether we are speaking, presenting or conversing. And he replicates this structure in thirty-seven speeches! By the time we get to the end of the book, that structure is ***well and truly rammed home and ingrained on our psyche!***

The speaking tips are great too. Most are of course well known to those of us with experience of speaking, but they are presented afresh and with Joe's quintessential vitality. And a number of them are novel. So too are the acronyms, which are many, memorable and often pertinent to the message – ***like speaking persuasively through BED-ding the audience!***

Above all, Joe demonstrates throughout the book the need for injecting light relief into almost every speech – the exception being speeches on very serious or sad issues. He does this by placing the elements of light relief in bold italics, so we can check once the speech is drafted that there are sufficient elements of bold italics placed strategically throughout it. This will be helpful in all types of speeches – ***including this evaluation!***

THE BODY: SUGGESTIONS

I have two main suggestions for Joe. The thirty-seven speeches do work as a book, but at times only just. There is no substitute for being there, for listening to the speech, for engaging with, even heckling the speaker. Joe's club members were lucky to have witnessed them live. But sometimes the text of a speech, along with its speaker instructions in brackets, comes over as a bit wooden. Some speeches, like those on vocal variety and body movement, are really best experienced live. Joe has videoed many of them and put them on YouTube, ***but perhaps he could get a move on and upload them all!***

The second suggestion is related. Some of the jokes or elements of light relief fall flat on the page. Some may well have bombed live too. I know what Joe would say to that: 'Look at sitcom comedians or stand-ups and tally what proportion of their gags come off; it doesn't matter; the important thing is the light relief, without which the speech risks becoming a lecture.' This is a fair point, especially when a speech is experienced live. ***But when a gag falls flat on the page, it falls flatter!***

THE BODY: COMPLETING THE PRAISE SANDWICH

But these suggestions pale in comparison to what the book achieves. The book guides us on speech structure through showing again and again how it is done and teaches us about speech content and delivery in memorable, understandable, often light-hearted mini-speeches. It is original, innovative and educative.

CONCLUSION

In summary, ladies and gentlemen, there are plenty of books on public speaking and any new book has to be viewed alongside Plato's judgement: 'Wise men speak because they have something to say. Fools because they have to say something.' ***Joe's no fool.***

Mr Chairman

SAMPLE SPEECHES AND NOTES

APPENDIX 1:
INFORMATIVE SPEECHES

KISSTRATEGY
by Vaughan Evans

Mr Chairman, ladies and gentlemen, how many of you here run your own business? Quite a few, that's good. For those who don't, here's a thought – imagine you are running a guest house in the West Country – or even on a Caribbean island! [SING] *'Oh, island in the sun . . . !'*

Back to grey, grim reality, this evening I'd like to talk about how you can develop a winning strategy for your business. But let me start with a quote from a famous businesswoman, one who triumphed in the ultra-competitive, vicious, cut-throat market . . . ***of marrying millionaires***. She was the 1930s screen siren, Mae West, and she once said: [AMERICAN ACCENT] *'I only like two kinds of men, domestic and imported.'* Of greater relevance to this speech, perhaps, she also quipped: *'A man's kiss is his signature.'*

There's another meaning to the word 'kiss'. It is an acronym, used by the US military for over fifty years, to affirm a fundamental principle in the design of military hardware, and it stands for . . . anyone? Yes, *Keep It Simple, Stupid*. It is my contention this evening that KISSTRATEGY should be the signature of a thriving business, of your business.

KISSTRATEGY is designed to keep strategy as simple as possible for the small business owner. It has just three core elements: understanding the market, creating competitive advantage and managing risk.

First you need to understand the market in which your business operates. How big is it? How fast is it growing? How tough is the competition? Is it getting tougher?

Take one extreme – entertainment retailing on the High Street. The likes of HMV, Zavvi and Woolworths were assaulted by virtually every negative competitive force conceivable. There were the new entrants, first the supermarkets, then the online retailers, like Amazon and

Play.com. Later on came the substitutes, like online downloading, initially with piracy, then iTunes, now Spotify. It became the competitive environment from hell. As the philosopher Jean Paul Sartre remarked in a somewhat different context: [FRENCH ACCENT] *'Hell . . . is other people.'*

Second: you need to create a competitive advantage. How well is your business placed relative to the competition? How can you strengthen your competitive position – and sustain your advantage?

Think on Facebook. It was developed by an undergraduate nerd trying to land himself a date. *He now has 1.5 billion friends to choose from.* It listed on the New York Stock Exchange a couple of years ago with a staggering price tag, which seemed to ignore the possibility of someone one day doing to Facebook what Facebook had done to MySpace. Did investors believe that Facebook's competitive advantage was indefinite? Yet it operates in a market with rapid technological change, low costs of start-up and negligible barriers to customer switching. And that's not counting the retro risk: when I was a lad, we had another phrase for social networking: *getting a life!*

Which brings us to the third element of KISSTRATEGY – managing risk. If your chosen strategy offers acceptable returns but at an unacceptable degree of risk, you may need to think again.

Take The Beatles. If you were a producer at Parlophone Records in 1963, would you have backed them? The risks were huge. A manager at Decca remarked famously at the time that Buddy Holly-style guitar groups were a thing of the past, a fad of the 1950s. And there were so many such groups around – the city of Liverpool alone had two dozen of them. These Beatle boys were rude, unruly, they didn't have particularly good voices and didn't – at the time – compose their own material. But they had charisma and a catchy name. You took a punt. Good call. *You got a ticket to ride! To Penny Lane!* You said: 'Money', [SING] *'that's what I want!'* And you didn't want it when you were sixty-four. You wanted it . . . anyone? Yup, [SING] *'Yesterday!'*

In summary, ladies and gentlemen, keep your strategy simple. Understand the market context, create competitive advantage and manage the risks. Let KISSTRATEGY be your signature. Back to that island in the sun, is your guest house one of a handful or one of a hundred? What is special about yours? Can you manage the risks of empty rooms off season, political unrest or a hurricane? Are those risks outshone by the opportunities of sun, sand and sea – and, of course, the reggae and calypso: [SING, HANDS UP, FOREFINGERS TO SKY, HIPS GYRATING!] *'feeling hot, hot, hot'!*

One final thought on the K-I-S-S theme: in 1940, Winston Churchill was advised by his officials that he should make more of an effort to befriend the leader of the Free French Army, General de Gaulle. Churchill replied: [CHURCHILLIAN ACCENT] 'That's fine, I'll be like a Frenchman and kiss him on both cheeks – *or, if you prefer, on all four!'*

Mr Chairman

© Vaughan Evans, 2014

NOTES

Developing a business strategy is quite a heavy subject matter. Not so heavy as some, like double-entry bookkeeping (see Speech 4!) or the Americans entering the Great War (Speech 27), but weighty enough.

That means that a speech on the subject delivered to a lay audience, as distinct from one given to, say, an audience of SME business owners, needs to take care to keep the audience engaged.

This speech does so in three ways. It conjures up an image of business not of metal bashing or pen pushing, but of palm trees, coral sands and turquoise seas – something that many (most?) in the audience can relate, even aspire to. It attempts to make the speech relevant to as many members of the audience as possible.

And it injects pockets of light relief – kicking off with the classic quips from Mae West in the opening and ending with a characteristic Churchill anecdote. It includes something light or thought provoking at the end of each of the three main elements of KISSTRATEGY in the main body of the speech. And, of course, the speaker seizes the opportunity to open his vocal cords, not just with some favourite Beatles numbers, but with a couple of evocative songs by Harry Belafonte and Arrow!

Third, it selects examples, of Woolworths, Facebook and The Beatles, that most people can relate to and find of interest.

The aims of the speech, as indeed preached throughout this book, are twofold – to inform and yet to entertain. The speaker aspires for members of the audience, whether lay or business folk, to emerge more informed about the essence of business strategy – while also, hopefully, having had a bit of a laugh.

THE ART OF COMMUNICATION
by Mike Silverman

Mr Chairman, ladies and gentlemen, you know how expressive Italian people are with their gestures? I was in Rome once and I was hopelessly lost. Then I saw an elderly lady walking along the road, burdened with four heavy shopping bags, one under each arm, one in each hand. So I went up to her and said 'Scusi, senora – dove Via Veneto, per favore?' Clearly unimpressed with my Italian and in the certain knowledge I was a foreigner, with an inconvenienced sigh she slowly and laboriously put down each bag in turn and then delivered a gesture, one that was silent, exaggerated, very Italian but universally understood [RAISE SHOULDERS TO EARS, LIFT HANDS TO THE HEAVENS].

Did I understand exactly what she was saying to me? Yes, I did [SHAKE HEAD IN THE NEGATIVE!]. Could there be any misunderstanding about her meaning? No, there couldn't [NOD HEAD IN THE AFFIRMATIVE!]. Are you confused by my gestures? Yes, you are [SHAKE MY HEAD IN THE NEGATIVE].

What I'm illustrating here is the power of gestures. On their own, they're usually perfectly explicit – but put them together with words without synchronicity and they have the power to confuse and mislead.

They may also be misinterpreted. There's an ancient story, from the time of the Spanish Inquisition. It tells of a band of gypsy people, who planned to make a permanent home outside the walls of a great city. But the King was not best pleased – he didn't want them there as they were not of the 'true faith' and so he banished them from his land.

The gypsies appealed and as the King was a fair man, he said, 'Very well, but they must earn the right to stay. I will challenge them to a debate with my archbishop – if they win, they may stay – if they lose, they must go.' But the King was also a crafty man and he set three conditions: the debate must be held without speaking; the representative of the gypsies must be a young boy; and the Archbishop alone would decide who won or who lost.

So, on the appointed day, a young gypsy boy appeared at court before the King and all his courtiers. The imposing figure of the Archbishop rose and started to communicate. He held up three fingers, whereupon the boy responded by holding up one finger. The Archbishop waved his hand in a circular motion above his head – and the boy responded by pointing at the floor next to him. The Archbishop then turned and fetched a bottle of wine and a wafer. The boy paused, reached into his pocket and pulled out an apple. The Archbishop thought for a moment and then turned to the King and said, 'I am defeated, the boy has won, the gypsies must stay!'

The boy left and the courtiers ran to the King, stunned at their defeat. The King asked angrily, 'What happened, what was said, how did you lose?' The Archbishop said, 'I began by saying [HOLD UP THREE FINGERS] we believe in the Trinity. The boy replied [HOLD UP ONE FINGER] there is but one god, whom we all share. I said [WAVE HAND IN A CIRCULAR MOTION ABOVE HEAD] God is all around us and the boy said [POINT AT THE FLOOR] he is right here beside him. Finally, I showed him the wine and a wafer as penance for our sins, whereupon he showed me an apple to remind me of the original sin. I knew then that this boy had an answer for everything and I could never win.'

Meanwhile, the boy went back to his gypsy camp and went immediately to his elders to tell them what happened. He said, 'The Bishop told me [HOLD UP THREE FINGERS] we have three days to get out.

I told him [HOLD UP ONE FINGER] not one of us is leaving. He said [WAVE HAND IN A CIRCULAR MOTION ABOVE HEAD] if you don't leave, the King will send his soldiers and clear you from his land. I replied [POINT AT THE FLOOR] we're staying right here.'

The boy paused. The elders said, 'Well, what happened next?' The boy said, 'I don't know. He took out his lunch, so I took out mine!'

So, perhaps gestures on their own are not so unequivocal – we need words <u>and</u> gestures in harmony.

Today I'm going to talk about the three most important factors that make for good communication. We've looked at the power of gestures, now we'll look at the single most important lesson I have learnt in many years of speaking in public: knowing your audience.

If you don't know your audience, you need to do your research and prepare accordingly. Here's what happens if you don't. I was once asked to give a talk to a large audience in Moscow. I thought it would be a nice idea to do the speech in Russian rather than English. I only had two weeks, so I took a crash course and that enabled me to understand enough Russian to be able to look at Russian words and annunciate them clearly enough.

So I wrote out my speech, had it translated into Russian and there I stood in front of an audience of five hundred, relaxed, confident and eager to show off my proficiency in their mother tongue. But just as I was about to start I realised I didn't know the Russian for 'ladies and gentlemen'. My host had told me a formal opening was required or the Russians would be offended. A wave of panic came over me as I desperately scanned the expectant audience.

My eyes came to rest on two signs at the back of the room and they gave me that vital burst of insight I so badly needed. Written above the two toilet doors in neon Cyrillic letters were the words 'buishwa' and 'tudadyeski' – obviously 'ladies' and 'gentlemen'.

I already knew the word for 'dear', 'doragai', so, delighted with my discovery and with renewed confidence, I launched into my speech with a resounding 'Doragai buishwa y tudadyeski' and proceeded to deliver what, if I say so myself, was a superb speech in flawless Russian.

At the cocktail party afterwards I asked my host how my speech had been received. He said, 'very well, your Russian is excellent, but we were a bit confused by your opening remarks.' 'Why?' I asked, 'I only said, "Dear ladies and gentlemen."' 'Unfortunately not,' he said 'what you said was "Dear urinals and water closets!"'

In the late 1990s my work took me frequently to Ireland and over the years I got to know the people of the Emerald Isle very well – including their unique sense of humour and 'sideways view of life'.

Like the time I was checking in at Heathrow to fly to Dublin. The gentleman in the queue right in front of me turned round and said 'I wish I'd brought me piano.' I asked him why and he replied, 'Because I left me ticket on it!'

On another trip I was invited to visit my colleague, Timothy, in a small town in County Kerry. It was a four-hour train journey from

Dublin and when I reached the station, I was told to walk into the town, find O'Reilly's pub and Timothy would be waiting for me with a pint of Guinness.

Well, I arrived at the station quite late at night to find that the town was some way from the station. Five miles, to be precise. It was pitch-black. There were neither street lights nor taxis. I walked and walked in the dark until I finally came across the town. I found O'Reilly's and there indeed was Timothy, waiting for me at the bar, along with my pint of Guinness.

'Hello, Michael,' he said cheerfully, 'you made good time.' I replied 'Maybe, Timothy, but that's an awful long way from the station to the town.' He nodded, 'So it is, Michael, so it is.' I asked 'Well, why didn't they build the station <u>in</u> the town?' And Timothy replied, 'They thought about that but decided it would be better by the railway line!'

The next day Timothy and I drove to Kinsale for a conference. We checked into a small pub-cum-b&b, dropped our bags off in our rooms and went to the bar. It was about three o'clock in the afternoon. I asked the landlady when was opening time – she said: 'That'll be five o'clock, my darling, but would you like a drink while you're waiting?'

I could carry on with stories like this until tomorrow. My point is this – humour is the great 'relaxant' – it relaxes your audience, which relaxes you – a virtuous circle! There are very few speeches, including eulogies, which would not benefit from a touch of humour. I try to get a laugh in the first thirty seconds of almost every speech I make. The only caveat when it comes to using humour is that it is never more important to 'know your audience' and to always choose humour that is 'appropriate and inclusive'.

In summary, these are the three main lessons I have learned that I believe make for good communication:

- Harnessing the power of gestures – and making sure they are in harmony with your words
- Knowing your audience, and
- Using humour at every available opportunity

Let me leave you with this thought, which trainers will tell you to be a myth, but I believe to be true: we only remember 10 per cent of what we hear, 20 per cent of what we see, but 50 per cent of what we hear <u>and</u> see.

Sorry, that was a very poor piece of communication. What I should have said was this:

We only remember this much [HOLD UP ONE FINGER] of what we hear; this much [HOLD UP TWO FINGERS] of what we see; but this much [HOLD UP FIVE FINGERS] of what we hear <u>and</u> see.

Mr Chairman

© Mike Silverman, 2014

NOTES

This is a work of joy – a joy of tales, of characters, of life. Mike grasps the opportunity – this was a workshop on communication – to stand up and tell some humorous, life-affirming, world-embracing tales – oh, yes, and, almost as a by-product, weave in a few lessons on the art of communication!

Mike's selection of tales is masterly. Each one illustrates clearly the point he is making, each is vivid and humorous and each causes no offence to anyone – except, perhaps, the inquisitorial Archbishop!

There is one area though where the speech could perhaps be improved and that is structure. Mike deploys a rather loose, free-form structure and the speech might benefit from one more rigorous, like that advocated throughout this book – a clear opening, body and conclusion (see Speech 6). Mike certainly has the conclusion – an emphatic restatement of the power of combining gestures with words. He has the body – three top tips on the art of communication.

But where is the opening? If the piece on gestures was the opening, it is a rather lengthy one – indeed it is half the speech! And are not gestures one of his three main lessons in communication, thereby slotting better into the body of the speech?

And the body would benefit from more signposting (Speech 7). The first time we get to hear Mike's three main tips on communicating is at the very end of the speech. A message is delivered more clearly if you tell us what you are going to tell us, tell us and then tell us what you told us. Mike opts for the latter alone!

But this is nit-picking. The purpose of Mike's talk was as much to entertain as inform, not to demonstrate how to build the perfectly structured speech.

And now and again you've just got to go with the flow. Character speakers write their own rules. Mike is such a delightful speaker, with his engaging stage presence, expressive vocal delivery and, his trademark, the all-embracing gestures, that as one glorious Italian, gypsy, Russian or Irish tale flows into another, almost as a one-man craic, who gives tuppence ha'penny about structure?!

PS By the way, did you note that Mike's lessons on the art of communication bear striking similarities to those espoused in this book? Anyone would think we were graduates of the same school of speaking . . . ?!

APPENDIX 2:
INSPIRATIONAL SPEECHES

JUST SO LUCKY
by Jock Elliott

Mr Chairman, ladies and gentlemen, if I joined Twitter or Facebook, I could have hundreds of brand new friends, just like that. But how many of them would roll out of bed at three o'clock in the morning and come to my aid if I needed them? Probably not one! So, who can I count on?

Well, I'm just so lucky because I have three best friends. And here they are: the friends of my blood, the friends of my times and the friends of my heart.

First, over here, the friends of my blood, that's my family! My mum and dad, my brother and sisters, my children. This is an old friendship, forged from birth, a lifelong link between my past and my future. Of course, we've had our differences, just like every family. But I'm just so lucky because we got over those. And anyway if you can't shout at your brother and sister, who can you shout at? And blood is thicker than water. And no one is thicker than my brother.

Now here, we have the friends of my times. Of school days and military service, of good times and bad times, of shared experience and common values. They're very important to me, but you'd like them too, because they think the way you do. They think, for example, that friends are the family you choose for yourself.

And finally here, we have the friends of my heart, of lovers. And for me that's my wife, Robyn. Now lovers are special kinds of friends because they're not imposed on us like family and school friends. Theirs is a friendship entered into gladly, willingly, joyfully, passionately. Sometimes in the springtime of life, when young blood courses through vibrant veins. Sometimes later in life, when more sluggish blood cruises . . . through varicose veins. My blood no longer courses, nor even cruises, it just coagulates. But I can still savour the richness of life with my wife, my lover, my companion, my friend for all my days.

Because, you see, this friendship of lovers can last for the rest of our lives. Or it may burn with the power of a sunburst, hot and bright and brief to fade and die, leaving two burnt-out husks, bitter and twisted and scarred. Been there, done that, got the T-shirt. Because sometimes love does fail. Without friendship, love cannot last. But with friendship, love can last forever. But like anything of value it must be earnt and maintained and we, we could all tell a thousand stories, each nothing in themselves but adding up together to something wonderful.

So, what kind of a friend am I? Do my friends get from me what I get from them? I've never told them, never told them the things I'm telling you. But I do freely give them advice they didn't asked for. I do give comfort when they need it. I do make them laugh when perhaps they'd rather cry. I'm always the same. I'm always there. That's all I've got. But it's all theirs.

My friends, you, the friends of my times, have now met my three best friends. But you all have these same friends. Different names, different faces, but in some form or another, these are the people who will roll out of bed at three o'clock in the morning and come to your aid because you need them. And they know that you'd do the same for them.

Tomorrow, we shall all be gone from here, scattering to our homes across the world. But before we go, taking with us perhaps some new friendships, let me just remind you that sitting next to you, right by your side, if you're lucky, may be the friend of your heart, or of your times, or of your blood.

Reach out now in your minds and hearts and touch them. Feel their warmth. Feel their friendship. Feel the ties that bind. And if we treasure these ties, nurture these ties, then we'll have all the luck we'll ever need. And we won't need Facebook.

Mr Chairman

© Jock Elliott, 2011 (www.jockelliott.com)

NOTES

This speech won Jock the World Championship of Public Speaking, 2011, so I hesitate before evaluating it. But what the heck . . . ?!

Jock's greatest asset is his rapport with the audience. The 'boy from Bongaree' looks like Mr Everyman, he sounds like Mr Everyman, his words are carefully chosen to be those of Mr Everyman. Thus Jock manages to cross the divide and enter the audience, to speak not to us, certainly not at us, but with us, even for us. He gets the audience to think and feel as he does.

Such a skill does not come easily, and not without practice. Jock jests that he was an 'overnight sensation', having won the World Championship after a mere 360 previous attempts! That included contests at club, area, division, district or international level – he was six times a world finalist – over a thirty-year career at Toastmasters.

I heard Jock give an illuminating seminar on how to construct a winning speech at a Toastmasters Conference in Dublin in May 2014. My three main takeaways were these:

- Make the speech meaningful – make what matters to you matter to them, otherwise you are being self-indulgent; give the audience something to take home, forever – 'a good speech is like a good book or a good song – it is memorable and creates an emotional connection'
- Handcraft the speech to perfection – every word must work, don't let the audience drift off, every word must be crafted, learnt off by heart, like a poem
- Blend the emotional with the light-hearted – pull the audience in with emotion, but be sure to release them again with some light relief, mix the schmaltz with the light, always strive for the balance

Applying these tips to Jock's speech shows just how he did it. The choice of topic is clever and inclusive – we all cherish friendships and Jock leaves us with the thought that we are 'just so lucky' to have them. The speech does indeed seem handcrafted – for example, his 'young blood courses through vibrant veins' or his immaculately spaced 'I'm always the same. I'm always there. That's all I've got. But it's all theirs.' And he blends the emotions of the audience masterfully – pausing dolefully over a presumed failure of his first marriage before bouncing back with a gag on giving friends advice they hadn't asked for.

My thoughts on how the speech could have been improved are twofold: more humour, some quotes. The overall balance of the speech was for my taste a bit too weighted towards the preachy, the trite and the schmaltzy, especially towards the end. I would have liked to have seen a couple more gags – like the one about his brother – or a meaty anecdote on friendship, whether personal or of a third party known to all.

Also the speech cried out for a quote or two – whether from the bible ('Greater love hath no man than this . . . '), Muhammad Ali ('Friendship is not something you learn at school . . . ') or Lennon and McCartney ('I get by with a little help from my friends'). Even better, we could have had Jock doing a Joe Cocker-style soul interpretation of the latter song on stage!

But Jock's speech won him the crown – and no doubt my recommendations would have lost it for him! Jock knew his audience – and his judges (see Speech 2), dressed immaculately (Speech 3), chose an embracing topic (Speech 4), structured the speech perfectly, topping and tailing it with the Facebook quip (Speech 6), lightened it as appropriate (Speech 8), personalised it throughout (Speech 9), delivered it impeccably (Part III) and applied the QED (qualifications, emotions, ditto) of an inspirational speech (Speech 27).

This was a champion speech from a champion speaker.

WE DON'T NEED ANOTHER HERO!
by Yvonne Jordan

[SING] 'We don't need another hero'! All right, I am no Tina Turner, but if only I had listened to those lyrics of hers back in 1985, it would have set me free, free to be me!

Back then I was still in school and had such high hopes, such dreams, and such a lot of goals! And according to our teachers, we couldn't have enough goals. It was goals, goals, goals! You would think we were fighting relegation from the first division! Let me share with you some of those goals and dreams . . .

I believed that my destination was to join the convent – I thought I had heard a calling! [PRODUCE SMALL MODEL OF CHURCH] Not just to become a nun, not just to be the Mother Superior, but to be . . . the new Mother Teresa!

I went to a convent school and as soon as you mentioned anything about becoming a nun it was immediately seized upon! I found myself in a car being driven at high speed to a convent 'open day' in the Midlands. I was sure the nuns in the Midlands would be thrilled to see my hilarious impersonations of the nuns back home in Enniscorthy! Wrong again! If we drove there fast, it was nothing like the speed we drove home, in silence. The chaplain turned to me and said: 'Yvonne, you might think you are ready for the convent but the convent is not ready for you.' Gone were my dreams of becoming a nun, joining the convent, being the new Mother Teresa. [TOSS CHURCH INTO BIN!]

Another of my dreams involved my favourite subject in school, art. I was particularly impressed with the impressionists, Monet, Manet and Degas. [PRODUCE FRAMED MONET PAINTING] I loved how the pastel colours melded together without heavy outline or form. Every time I looked at these paintings I felt such joy and so uplifted. I thought that's it! I'll become a famous artist! I sketched, I drew, I painted, I created . . . landfill! [TOSS PAINTING INTO BIN!]

Having left school, I knew that money was not everything, but I also knew that everything cost money. I had a thought, not exactly an original thought: [SING] 'All the things I could do, if I had a little money'. Thank you, Abba, for the financial advice, but I had my own plan! I went to the library and got out all the 'How to get rich quick' books I could get my hands on. [PRODUCE BOOKS] My plan was simple – I was going to take all the best ideas from the books, amalgamate them, and come up with my own foolproof, how to get rich quick plan. Well, it certainly fooled me! [TOSS BOOKS INTO BIN!]

I left college and far from feeling like a hero I felt like a failure. I felt I was at best average, mediocre, just an everyday sort of person. But, you will be glad to know I rallied again. Now, granted it took almost fifteen years to establish a new set of goals, realistic goals, goals for the rest of my life.

I decided if I am average, I'll try to be A+ at average. If I am mediocre, I will be marvellous at mediocrity, and excel at the everyday!

And who better to help me than those from my dismissed dreams? Each day I have a Mother Teresa moment, where I try to do one selfless act, to make someone else's day a little bit better. My Mother Teresa moment! [RETRIEVE CHURCH FROM BIN!]

I work as an interior designer, and do a lot of visual displays where I try to create something beautiful, to bring a bit of beauty into the world. That's my Monet moment! [RETRIEVE PAINTING FROM BIN!]

Then there's the 'How to get rich' books. [RETRIEVE BOOK FROM BIN, PONDER, FIRE IT BACK IN BIN!] They still don't work – but I do work at excelling at the everyday tasks. I was the sort of person who packed the dishwasher by standing a metre back and lobbing the stuff in, and nonchalantly kicking the door as I passed – then wondering why the stuff came out dirtier an hour later. Now I take the time to do it right, excel at the everyday!

Richard Attenborough once said: 'We all need heroes, to measure our own shortcomings by.' I say: thank you, Richard, but stick to the films! I don't want to measure my own shortcomings! Tina Turner was right, we don't need another hero! Thankfully I have reached a stage in my life where I am just happy being me!

Mr Chairman

NOTES

This speech won Yvonne the 2012 Britain and Ireland public speaking championship. I wasn't there, but I can picture it.

I saw Yvonne give a speech on emotional intelligence at the finals a couple of years later and she blew me away. She has an electric presence on stage. She stands confidently but not cockily, she looks fabulous but not flashy and she delivers her lines in a warm, engaging Irish lilt, replete with the variety of pace and pitch of a trained actress – though that she is not.

This speech is well targeted. Her tales of the convent will have resonated with the Irish half of the audience, while her selection of songs from the 1980s befits a mean audience age of around forty-five. Very few people in that audience would have been unfamiliar with Tina Turner or Abba!

The speech is all about her. This is high risk. If she had not captured the audience with her presence, charm and vitality it would have bombed. But it went down a treat, according to those who were there, and she scooped the crown.

As with any speech, however, there may be room for improvement, perhaps in three areas. Although it is clever to drop in the name of Mother Teresa, maybe four times is a bit much?! After all, half of the audience would have been British and mainly non-Catholic.

I think the final quarter of the speech fizzles out a bit. It seems a bit contrived. Yvonne's Mother Teresa and Monet moments are clever, but only leave us looking forward to a similar moment connected with how to get rich quick. Excelling at loading the dishwasher doesn't quite hack it!

Finally, the end needs a bit more of a bang. Perhaps just a couple of extra short sentences could do it, for example, in italics: 'Tina Turner was right, we don't need another hero! *And I don't want to be a hero. Not me, not anymore.* I am happy just being me!'

I love the patches of humour throughout the speech. I can imagine Yvonne's long pause before . . . 'landfill'! And I can picture her putting on a deep chaplain's voice and admonishing herself!

Even without the props, this would have been a winning speech. The props put the icing on the cake. They were handmade – the church out of an orange juice carton and cornflake box, Blue Peter-esque, sprayed silver, and the Monet painted by Yvonne's own hand. Their initial revelation, subsequent binning and ultimate resurrection are vivid master strokes.

A stellar speech, delivered by a star.

LIFE IS IN THE LIVING OF IT
by Vaughan Evans

I wake up, well, sort of. My eyes are sticky, my mouth dry, my head throbbing madly, the inevitable consequences of innumerable shots of *tuak*, the sickly sweet rice wine beloved of the Dayaks.

I am in a longhouse, lying on a rattan mat on the slatted bamboo floor. I become aware that *I am stark naked*. And not just me – *so too is my new friend, the daughter of the Dayak chief*, lying beside me, still unconscious. Well, she isn't entirely naked. *While asleep, she has had feathers glued in strategic locations*. I have been similarly attended to – *attached to my most private part, rather too tightly, is a piece of string. The other end of the string is tied to a leg, belonging to a large, brown, furry spider, about the size of a child's fist*.

It was probably the spider that woke me up – *it was frisky, and rather ticklish*. Or perhaps it was the cacophony, *coming from the assembly of Dayak men and women sitting cross-legged in a circle around the two of us*, all hooting with laughter at my evident discomfort and embarrassment. What to do? I sat up, grinned and demanded: *'tuak lagi' – more tuak!*

Mr Chairman, ladies and gentlemen, this was 1980 and I was living in Sarawak, northern Borneo. I had landed on a tiny grass airstrip deep in the rainforest, followed by a six-hour barge ride upriver, to discover a picture-perfect, palm-fronted longhouse. I showed up as a total stranger, but was welcomed immediately by the longhouse community into their extraordinary harvest festival of Gawai – a bacchanal of dancing, singing, loving, eating, drinking and vomiting – *and mischievous trickery on anyone foolish enough to pass out!*

I spent twelve years living and working in tropical lands, in the Caribbean, the South Pacific and South-East Asia, and my philosophy in those days was simple: life is in the living of it. This was taken direct from the character Pierre in Tolstoy's *War and Peace*, who struggles for years to find the meaning of life, before sharing a barracks in a prisoner-of-war camp with common soldiers and discovering that the secret of life lies not in the thinking of it, but in the doing of it, the living of it.

In later life, pursuing that philosophy becomes tougher. We develop commitments, especially when a family comes along. We fight to hold onto our jobs, or keep our businesses afloat. We get bogged down by loans, mortgages, insurances, pensions, all designed to strip the fun out of living for today. We become like Homer Simpson: *'What's the point of going out? We're just gonna wind up back here anyway!'*

But it is just about possible to hang on to that philosophy. Richard Branson, after a lifetime of taking on new challenges, has been pioneering space tourism – and, despite severe setbacks, still intends to be on the maiden voyage. Back to earth, or rather water, my brother-in-law, a retired surgeon, has bought a yacht and is preparing to sail it round the world, *dragging my long-suffering, land-loving sister in his wake!* Life is in the living of it – *at least for him!*

Back to the longhouse. I had arrived late afternoon on a Friday, and the following Monday morning, I managed to drag myself up at the crack of dawn to catch the early morning barge back downriver. I was threading my way down the notched log [WALK AS ON TIGHTROPE] leading from the longhouse to the riverbank when the barge came chugging round the river bend. I waved to the skipper to get him to pull up but as I did so I slipped on the damp log and *landed flat on my back in 12 inches of red mud*. The barge chugged blindly by. What to do? I picked myself up, squelched back up to the longhouse and demanded: *'tuak lagi!'*

The next morning, I somehow managed to keep my footing on the notched log, caught the barge and eventually the light aircraft and that night I was back in my apartment in the capital, Kuching. I showed up tentatively at the office the next morning and, to my surprise, my boss wasn't angry at all. He seemed delighted to see me. I soon found out why. *It wasn't a Wednesday, but a Thursday*. Having slipped off that notched log, I wasn't just a day late back in the office, but two days late. *He had had visions of me simmering away in a large cooking pot!*

Ladies and gentlemen, you may think that this story just proves the old maxim that if you are going to be late, be very late. But to me, having lost a whole day of my life to oblivion, *to warm-hearted, whacky, wonderful oblivion*, it seemed the perfect example of my enduring philosophy: *Life is in the living of it!*

Mr Chairman

© Vaughan Evans, 1990 and 2014

NOTES

This is an example of wrapping a message around a story. Clearly the speaker wanted to tell the audience of a remarkable tale (and largely true – the spider wasn't that big, but, believe me, big enough!) that happened to him many years before.

But if the speech had just been a tale, how would that have engaged the audience? Better to wrap the tale inside a philosophy consistent with and relevant to the tale – and one that may strike a chord with many.

Had the speech been written the other way round, with the primary objective of sharing that philosophical and inspirational message, the structure would have been different. The introduction would have centred around the message and the body of the speech given to two or three angles or anecdotes that supported the message, one of which being the tale of the Gawai festival at the Dayak longhouse.

That would have been equally valid, and might indeed have worked better, but in truth that was not the main purpose. This was my maiden speech to a new club and the main objective was simply to introduce myself. I chose to do so by sharing an extraordinary experience – a few days so hedonistically befuddled that one of them became lost to memory forever!

APPENDIX 3:
MOTIVATIONAL SPEECHES

ACCEPTING THE NOBEL PRIZE FOR PEACE
by His Holiness The Dalai Lama

Your Majesty, Members of the Nobel Committee, Brothers and Sisters.

I am very happy to be here with you today to receive the Nobel Prize for Peace. I feel honoured, humbled and deeply moved that you should give this important prize to a simple monk from Tibet. I am no one special. But I believe the prize is a recognition of the true value of altruism, love, compassion and non-violence which I try to practise, in accordance with the teachings of the Buddha and the great sages of India and Tibet.

I accept the prize with profound gratitude on behalf of the oppressed everywhere and for all those who struggle for freedom and work for world peace. I accept it as a tribute to the man who founded the modern tradition of non-violent action for change – Mahatma Gandhi – whose life taught and inspired me. And, of course, I accept it on behalf of the six million Tibetan people, my brave countrymen and women inside Tibet, who have suffered and continue to suffer so much. They confront a calculated and systematic strategy aimed at the destruction of their national and cultural identities. The prize reaffirms our conviction that with truth, courage and determination as our weapons Tibet will be liberated.

No matter what part of the world we come from, we are all basically the same human beings. We all seek happiness and try to avoid suffering. We have the same basic human needs and concerns. All of us human beings want freedom and the right to determine our own destiny as individuals and as peoples. That is human nature. The great changes that are taking place everywhere in the world, from Eastern Europe to Africa, are a clear indication of this.

In China the popular movement for democracy was crushed by

brutal force in June this year. But I do not believe the demonstrations were in vain, because the spirit of freedom was rekindled among the Chinese people and China cannot escape the impact of this spirit of freedom sweeping many parts of the world. The brave students and their supporters showed the Chinese leadership and the world the human face of that great nation.

Last week a number of Tibetans were once again sentenced to prison terms of up to nineteen years at a mass show trial, possibly intended to frighten the population before today's event. Their only 'crime' was the expression of the widespread desire of Tibetans for the restoration of their beloved country's independence.

The suffering of our people during the past forty years of occupation is well documented. Ours has been a long struggle. We know our cause is just. Because violence can only breed more violence and suffering, our struggle must remain non-violent and free of hatred. We are trying to end the suffering of our people, not to inflict suffering upon others.

It is with this in mind that I proposed negotiations between Tibet and China on numerous occasions. In 1987, I made specific proposals in a Five-Point plan for the restoration of peace and human rights in Tibet. This included the conversion of the entire Tibetan plateau into a Zone of Ahimsa, a sanctuary of peace and non-violence where human beings and nature can live in peace and harmony.

Last year, I elaborated on that plan in Strasbourg at the European Parliament. I believe the ideas I expressed on those occasions are both realistic and reasonable, although they have been criticised by some of my people as being too conciliatory. Unfortunately, China's leaders have not responded positively to the suggestions we have made, which included important concessions. If this continues we will be compelled to reconsider our position.

Any relationship between Tibet and China will have to be based on the principle of equality, respect, trust and mutual benefit. It will also have to be based on the principle which the wise rulers of Tibet and of China laid down in a treaty as early as 823 AD, carved on the pillar which still stands today in front of the Jokhang, Tibet's holiest shrine, in Lhasa, that 'Tibetans will live happily in the great land of Tibet, and the Chinese will live happily in the great land of China.'

As a Buddhist monk, my concern extends to all members of the human family and, indeed, to all sentient beings who suffer. I believe all suffering is caused by ignorance. People inflict pain on others in the selfish pursuit of their happiness or satisfaction. Yet true happiness comes from a sense of brotherhood and sisterhood. We need to cultivate a universal responsibility for one another and the planet we share. Although I have found my own Buddhist religion helpful in generating love and compassion, even for those we consider our enemies, I am convinced that everyone can develop a good heart and a sense of universal responsibility with or without religion.

With the ever growing impact of science on our lives, religion and spirituality have a greater role to play in reminding us of our humanity. There is no contradiction between the two. Each gives us valuable insights into the other. Both science and the teachings of the Buddha tell us of the fundamental unity of all things. This understanding is crucial if we are to take positive and decisive action on the pressing global concern with the environment.

I believe all religions pursue the same goals, that of cultivating human goodness and bringing happiness to all human beings. Though the means might appear different the ends are the same.

As we enter the final decade of this century I am optimistic that the ancient values that have sustained mankind are today reaffirming themselves to prepare us for a kinder, happier twenty-first century.

I pray for all of us, oppressor and friend, that together we succeed in building a better world through human understanding and love, and that in doing so we may reduce the pain and suffering of all sentient beings.

Thank you.

NOTES

This is wonderful motivational speech, cast cleverly and tactfully under the cloak of an inspirational speech. It inspires those in the audience and beyond to work together peacefully towards mutual understanding, harmony and happiness. And it works perfectly on that level.

But the underlying message is to motivate the Tibetan people to remain strong, to carry on their fight, peacefully but persistently, for freedom.

The motivational aspect of the speech subtly uses the CAP techniques, of culture, ardour and progress (see Speech 28), to perfection. The Tibetans in the audience will be reminded of their sacred culture by reference to the Jokhang temple. Their ardour will be aroused by the ancient inscription on the pillar, since ingrained into their very being, that Tibetans will live happily in their own land.

Finally the speech raises hope by demonstrating progress, on two fronts. The Dalai Lama portrays the ruthless extermination of dissent in Tiananmen Square as one of the last gasps of a decadent regime. And he talks optimistically about his own five-year plan and proposals for a Zone of Ahimsa.

He even throws in after the carrot a little bit of stick about the possibility of the Tibetan people having to reconsider their position.

This is a masterful speech, one of inspiration and motivation, worthy even of his mentor, Mahatma Gandhi.

REACH YOUR NEW YEAR'S GOALS
IN FOUR EASY STEPS
by Brian Tracy

Thank you very much for watching. I want to explain to you what you can do to make 2015 the very best year of your life.

Your most valuable financial asset according to the research is your earning power, what is also called your human capital, or your intellectual property. It represents your skills and your ability to do stuff and get results that people will pay you for. And if you really want to make next year and the year after and the year after that wonderful years in your life financially what you have to do is to constantly increase your earning power.

I sometimes use this analogy on the stage: I say imagine climbing a ladder. You start off on the bottom rung at the beginning of your career and most people have no earning ability, but after ten or twenty years some people have climbed way higher than others, earning fifty times as much. And yet they started off at the same place.

The difference is that the top people learn new skills continually as they go through their career. They climb the ladder of success. Each new skill increases your ability to get results, it increases the value of your contribution.

Sometimes I ask my audience: 'How many people here work on straight commission?' And maybe 10 or 15 per cent of people will raise their hands. And then I point out: 'No, everybody works on commission.' Everybody works on a percentage of the value that they create. If you want to earn more money, create more value. It's as simple as that. Get more results. And the only way you can get results in the knowledge age, the age of the mind, is by learning and applying new skills that enable you to get more and better results, so that people will pay you more and more.

So how do you make 2015 a better year? First, set very clear goals for yourself. Exactly where do you want to be in twelve months? I always encourage my audience to take a sheet of paper and write down ten goals for the next twelve months. Then look at those goals and ask yourself if you could wave a magic wand and achieve any one goal from that list of ten which one goal would have the greatest, most positive impact on your life?

Now for most of us it's a financial goal. For some it may be a physical goal or a relationship goal or a business goal, but for most of us it is financial. Well, if it's a financial goal, write it down very clearly and set a date and make a list of everything you need to do to achieve that goal.

And the second question you ask is what one skill will help you the most to achieve that goal? Think of all the skills that you have – and if you're not clear, by the way, you must become clear. Ask your boss, look around you, look at the people who are earning the kind of money that you want to earn and find out the one skill that they have – and you need. We call this like the sniper school – one shot, one kill. You don't try to learn a whole bunch of skills, you focus on learning the one skill that can help you the most to achieve your most important goal.

This formula is an incredible formula, based on twenty-five years of research, and it's the reason why people go from the bottom to the top. They are first of all very focused on where they want to go and they are very clear on what skill they need to climb at each rung on the ladder. Each new rung on the ladder takes you up higher and increases your earning ability. As you increase your earning ability you open up new opportunities for yourself. The next rung up needs one more skill. You keep adding skills: you keep adding the most important skill that will help you achieve your most important goal.

Now on top of these two things you have to manage your time really well. Today we are overwhelmed with too much to do and too little time. So what you have to do is to plan every day in advance. And the simplest technique of all is a piece of paper, a pen and a few minutes of your time. Sometimes we say that if you want to invest your money your goal is to get the highest return on your investment. But if you are going to invest your energy in your career you need to get the highest return on that energy, on your mental and physical and emotional energy. Some people work all day and make a few dollars. Some people work all day and make hundreds of thousands of dollars.

Which one do you want to be? So manage your time by making a list of everything you have to do in the coming day and then go down over your list and ask if you could do just one thing on this list today before being called out of town which one would have the greatest value in your work? Which one item would help you the most to achieve your most important goal and achieve the highest possible income? Then start work on that one task. Don't check your email or play with your Smartphone or check your messages and so on, just put your head down, focus single-mindedly on one task, the most important task, and then work on it until it is 100 per cent complete.

I just heard a US Army General Chief of Staff who gave a commencement speech at a university and he talked about how in the military they teach you how to get out of bed and turn round and make your bed, completely, so that it will pass the inspection. He said what they are teaching people is to start and complete one task first thing in the morning. And this is one of the great psychological tricks of success. Start and complete a task first thing in the morning. Now if you're going to complete a task, start and complete an <u>important</u> task and do that every single day before you do anything else. Repeat this over and over again for three to four weeks and soon it becomes a habit. You wake up in the morning and you start work on your most important task.

In summary, if you want to reach your New Year's goals, here are four easy steps on how to do it: 1) determine your most important goal; 2) determine the most important skill that you can develop to achieve the goal; 3) plan each day in advance, and 4) determine the most important thing you can do each day to achieve your most important goal and then start and finish with that. These four steps alone will make you one of the most productive and highest paid people in our society.

They can help you make 2015 the very best year of your life.

Thank you for watching.

© Brian Tracy, December 2014 (www.briantracy.com)

NOTES

This is a succinct, informative and highly motivating speech from the renowned success guru. Brian has put into it some key observations and insights from his years of experience and delivered them to his audience cleverly and opportunely in the form of New Year resolutions.

It is not strictly speaking a speech. It is a video talk of six and a half minutes duration, posted online to Brian's many hundreds of thousands of e-newsletter subscribers and social media followers.

It is also by no means a scripted speech. Brian plans all his talks, but doesn't script them. He delivers them in a planned order, with planned headlines, but fills in the balance, the vast bulk of the talk, off the cuff. This is not surprising, since Brian delivers dozens of talks, seminars and workshops live each year, all over the world (he has spoken to more than 5 million people in 5,000 talks in over 50 countries!) – let alone the video clips he makes each week for the web. He cannot be expected to prepare and remember scripts for each, on a diverse range of motivational topics, ranging from goal-setting to leadership, maximum achievement to business planning (in which, in the spirit of disclosure, he co-wrote a book with this author).

Nevertheless, the video talk above has a simple structure – a brief opening, four steps and a succinct conclusion. And it is packed with self-developing content. His audience knows that he has a book or ten to back up his observations on each of the four steps he recommends on reaching goals.

I like the way Brian uses repetition in key passages of the talk to reinforce a point. Thus, for example: 'The next rung up needs one more skill. You keep adding skills: you keep adding the most important skill that will help you achieve your most important goal.' The most important messages in any speech benefit from being hammered home, but especially in a motivational speech. In this case Brian is telling us to focus on the one key skill needed to achieve the one key goal on each rung of the ladder. He delivers this, in an unscripted, extemporary way, powerfully.

Were we to treat this as a prepared, scripted speech, I would have two main recommendations. First, we could have done with a bit more signposting (see Speech 7). We only learn what the four steps needed to reach our goals are in the conclusion – some viewers, like myself, would have liked to have known what those steps were right up-front.

Also I think the 'speech' would have been more powerful with just three steps – this would not just have exploited the 'power of three' (Speech 7 again), but also the omission of Step 3 might have simplified and fortified the message. Thus the takeaway would have been: determine your most important goal; determine the most important skill that you can develop to achieve the goal; and determine the most important thing you can do each day to build that skill, hence achieve the goal.

But this is unfair: it was not a prepared, scripted speech – it was one of hundreds of videos and talks Brian delivers each year with just headline notes and no script. And the video succeeds in its purpose, conveying a simple, upbeat, motivating message for the viewer to kick off the New Year with.

Finally, and digressing from the speech itself to the speaker, it is illuminating to compare Brian's speaking style with that of the other pre-eminent motivational speaker of our age, Tony

Robbins. Their styles are very different, reinforcing the point I made earlier (see Speech 16) on how we should develop our own speaking style, based on our own personality, presence and vocal repertoire. Tony Robbins, with his deep, resonant voice and dramatic presence, is all about energy, fervour and passion. Brian's style is distinguished, warm, sincere, paternal, yet vital. Both are extraordinary communicators, but in their own distinct ways.

Watch clips of both on YouTube. Which is closest to your style? Or is yours different again and distinctive in its own right? Whichever, stick with your style, embrace it, develop it!

FUNERAL ORATIONS OF BRUTUS
AND MARK ANTONY FOR JULIUS CAESAR
by William Shakespeare

Brutus to the people

Romans, countrymen, and lovers! Hear me for my cause, and be silent that you may hear. Believe me for mine honour, and have respect to mine honour that you may believe. Censure me in your wisdom, and awake your senses that you may the better judge. If there be any in this assembly, any dear friend of Caesar's, to him I say that Brutus' love to Caesar was no less than his. If then that friend demand why Brutus rose against Caesar, this is my answer: not that I loved Caesar less, but that I loved Rome more.

Had you rather Caesar were living and die all slaves, than that Caesar were dead, to live all free men? As Caesar loved me, I weep for him. As he was fortunate, I rejoice at it. As he was valiant, I honour him. But, as he was ambitious, I slew him. There is tears for his love, joy for his fortune, honour for his valour, and death for his ambition. Who is here so base that would be a bondman? If any, speak – for him have I offended. Who is here so rude that would not be a Roman? If any, speak – for him have I offended. Who is here so vile that will not love his country? If any, speak – for him have I offended. I pause for a reply.

Then none have I offended. I have done no more to Caesar than you shall do to Brutus. The question of his death is enrolled in the Capitol. His glory not extenuated wherein he was worthy, nor his offences enforced for which he suffered death.

Here comes his body, mourned by Mark Antony, who, though he had no hand in his death, shall receive the benefit of his dying – a place in the commonwealth – as which of you shall not? With this I depart: that, as I slew my best lover for the good of Rome, I have the same dagger for myself when it shall please my country to need my death.

Mark Antony to the people

Friends, Romans, countrymen, lend me your ears.
I come to bury Caesar, not to praise him.
The evil that men do lives after them;
The good is oft interred with their bones.
So let it be with Caesar. The noble Brutus
Hath told you Caesar was ambitious.
If it were so, it was a grievous fault,
And grievously hath Caesar answered it.
Here, under leave of Brutus and the rest –
For Brutus is an honourable man;
So are they all, all honourable men –
Come I to speak in Caesar's funeral.

He was my friend, faithful and just to me.
But Brutus says he was ambitious,
And Brutus is an honourable man.

He hath brought many captives home to Rome
Whose ransoms did the general coffers fill.
Did this in Caesar seem ambitious?
When that the poor have cried, Caesar hath wept.
Ambition should be made of sterner stuff.
Yet Brutus says he was ambitious,
And Brutus is an honourable man.

You all did see that on the Lupercal
I thrice presented him a kingly crown,
Which he did thrice refuse. Was this ambition?
Yet Brutus says he was ambitious,
And, sure, he is an honourable man.

I speak not to disprove what Brutus spoke,
But here I am to speak what I do know.
You all did love him once, not without cause.
What cause withholds you then to mourn for him?

O judgement! Thou art fled to brutish beasts,
And men have lost their reason. Bear with me.
My heart is in the coffin there with Caesar,
And I must pause till it come back to me. [WEEPS]

[PLEBEIANS SPEAK]

But yesterday the word of Caesar might
Have stood against the world. Now lies he there,
And none so poor to do him reverence.
O masters, if I were disposed to stir
Your hearts and minds to mutiny and rage,
I should do Brutus wrong, and Cassius wrong –
Who, you all know, are honourable men.
I will not do them wrong. I rather choose
To wrong the dead, to wrong myself and you,
Than I will wrong such honourable men.

But here's a parchment with the seal of Caesar.
I found it in his closet. 'Tis his will.
Let but the commons hear this testament –
Which, pardon me, I do not mean to read –
And they would go and kiss dead Caesar's wounds
And dip their napkins in his sacred blood,
Yea, beg a hair of him for memory,
And, dying, mention it within their wills,
Bequeathing it as a rich legacy
Unto their issue.

[PLEBEIANS SPEAK]

Have patience, gentle friends. I must not read it.
It is not meet you know how Caesar loved you.
You are not wood, you are not stones, but men.
And, being men, bearing the will of Caesar,
It will inflame you, it will make you mad.
'Tis good you know not that you are his heirs.

For, if you should – Oh, what would come of it!

[PLEBEIANS SPEAK]

Will you be patient? Will you stay awhile?
I have o'ershot myself to tell you of it.
I fear I wrong the honourable men
Whose daggers have stabbed Caesar. I do fear it.

[PLEBEIANS SPEAK]

You will compel me, then, to read the will?
Then make a ring about the corpse of Caesar,
And let me show you him that made the will.

[PLEBEIANS SPEAK]

If you have tears, prepare to shed them now.
You all do know this mantle. I remember
The first time ever Caesar put it on.
'Twas on a summer's evening in his tent,
That day he overcame the Nervii.
Look, in this place ran Cassius' dagger through.
See what a rent the envious Casca made.
Through this the well-belovèd Brutus stabbed.
And as he plucked his cursèd steel away,
Mark how the blood of Caesar followed it,
As rushing out of doors, to be resolved
If Brutus so unkindly knocked, or no.
For Brutus, as you know, was Caesar's angel.
Judge, O you gods, how dearly Caesar loved him!
This was the most unkindest cut of all.
For when the noble Caesar saw him stab,
Ingratitude, more strong than traitors' arms,
Quite vanquished him. Then burst his mighty heart,
And, in his mantle muffling up his face,
Even at the base of Pompey's statue,
Which all the while ran blood, great Caesar fell.

O, what a fall was there, my countrymen!
Then I, and you, and all of us fell down,
Whilst bloody treason flourished over us.
Oh, now you weep, and, I perceive, you feel
The dint of pity. These are gracious drops.
Kind souls, what, weep you when you but behold
Our Caesar's vesture wounded? Look you here,
Here is himself, marred, as you see, with traitors.
[LIFTS UP CAESAR'S MANTLE]

[PLEBEIANS SPEAK]

Good friends, sweet friends! Let me not stir you up
To such a sudden flood of mutiny.
They that have done this deed are honourable.
What private griefs they have, alas, I know not,
That made them do it. They are wise and honourable,
And will, no doubt, with reasons answer you.
I come not, friends, to steal away your hearts.
I am no orator, as Brutus is,
But, as you know me all, a plain blunt man
That love my friend. And that they know full well
That gave me public leave to speak of him.
For I have neither wit nor words nor worth,
Action nor utterance nor the power of speech,
To stir men's blood. I only speak right on.
I tell you that which you yourselves do know,
Show you sweet Caesar's wounds, poor poor dumb mouths,
And bid them speak for me. But were I Brutus,
And Brutus Antony, there were an Antony
Would ruffle up your spirits and put a tongue
In every wound of Caesar that should move
The stones of Rome to rise and mutiny.

[PLEBEIANS SPEAK]

Why, friends, you go to do you know not what.
Wherein hath Caesar thus deserved your loves?
Alas, you know not. I must tell you then.
You have forgot the will I told you of.

[PLEBEIANS SPEAK]

Here is the will, and under Caesar's seal
To every Roman citizen he gives –
To every several man – seventy-five drachmas.

[PLEBEIANS SPEAK]

Moreover, he hath left you all his walks,
His private arbours and new-planted orchards,
On this side Tiber. He hath left them you
And to your heirs forever – common pleasures,
To walk abroad and recreate yourselves.
Here was a Caesar! When comes such another?

NOTES

It is humbling to read again these words. The scene of these mighty soldier politicians addressing the Roman people in the majestic Forum in front of the blooded, toga-shredded corpse of Julius Caesar is poignant enough. But the beauty of Shakespeare's words and the persuasive power within the rhetoric are breathtaking.

The art of rhetoric, or persuasive speaking, was a pillar of Western education from classical times through to the nineteenth century. An Elizabethan audience would have appreciated the nuances of these masterful speeches more so than an audience of today.

But one thing remains clear: despite the brilliance of Brutus's speech, Mark Antony's would have won the day. Why?

Shakespeare crafted the speeches as he imagined they would have been in Roman times. The rhetoric of the day followed Aristotle's three pillars of ethos, logos and pathos, in that order. Ethos (Greek for 'character') establishes the speaker's authority and expertise, ensuring that the audience will listen. Logos ('word') sets out the reason, the logic, and argues the case for the desired action. And pathos ('suffering') evokes the emotional connection, making the audience care about the action.

Neither speaker had to strive too hard with the ethos. The audience would have been well aware that Brutus was Caesar's chosen one, his 'angel' in the words of Mark Antony. And they knew Mark Antony as the blunt, reliable, victorious warrior, Caesar's second-in-command in the four-year civil war against Pompey.

Brutus sets out the logos ruthlessly. Caesar was an icon, but had become too ambitious. Brutus loved Caesar, but loved Rome more. He did to Caesar what he would expect Rome to do to him if he were to become as Caesar.

But Mark Antony dismisses Brutus's logos by revealing that Caesar had turned down the offer of a crown on three occasions. Was that the action of an ambitious man?

Then Mark Antony deploys the pathos card. He, the mighty soldier, weeps at the side of the corpse and cries that he would be stirred to 'mutiny and rage' were not the tragic deed carried out by such 'honourable' men – and Mark Antony would rather harm himself than harm such 'honourable' men!

He describes the deed itself in graphic, lyrical tones. He opens with an emotional 'If you have tears, prepare to shed them now' and shows the people the very cloak that Caesar first wore after a famous victory, but now blood-smeared and gashed with the, wait for it, 'poor poor dumb mouths' of the knife thrusts – wow!

Finally he pulls the ace from his sleeve and invokes the self-interest of his audience. He teases them to force him to read out Caesar's will, whereupon he reveals that Caesar has bequeathed much of his wealth and land to them, the Roman people. Could this be the will of a self-serving tyrant?

This is a persuasive speech of perfection, crafted by genius.

THE IRAQ CRISIS (EXCERPTS)
by Tony Blair

I beg to move the motion standing on the order paper in my name and those of my right honourable friends.

[About the tough but democratic choice before Parliament]
[About Saddam Hussein's game playing over UN WMD inspections, until faced with the threat of force]
[About the comparison with Hitler in the 1930s]

The threat today is not that of the 1930s. It's not big powers going to war with each other. The ravages which fundamentalist political ideology inflicted on the twentieth century are memories. The Cold War is over. Europe is at peace, if not always diplomatically.

But the world is ever more interdependent. Stock markets and economies rise and fall together. Confidence is the key to prosperity. Insecurity spreads like contagion. So people crave stability and order.

The threat is chaos. And there are two begetters of chaos. Tyrannical regimes with WMD and extreme terrorist groups who profess a perverted and false view of Islam.

Let me tell the House what I know. I know that there are some countries or groups within countries that are proliferating and trading in WMD, especially nuclear weapons technology.

I know there are companies, individuals, some former scientists on nuclear weapons programmes, selling their equipment or expertise.

I know there are several countries – mostly dictatorships with highly repressive regimes – desperately trying to acquire chemical weapons, biological weapons or, in particular, nuclear weapons capability.

Some of these countries are now a short time away from having a serviceable nuclear weapon. This activity is not diminishing. It is increasing.

We all know that there are terrorist cells now operating in most major countries. Just as in the last two years, around twenty different nations have suffered serious terrorist outrages. Thousands have died in them.

The purpose of terrorism lies not just in the violent act itself. It is in producing terror. It sets out to inflame, to divide, to produce consequences which they then use to justify further terror.

Round the world it now poisons the chances of political progress: in the Middle East; in Kashmir; in Chechnya; in Africa.

The removal of the Taliban in Afghanistan dealt it a blow. But it has not gone away.

And these two threats have different motives and different origins but they share one basic common view: they detest the freedom, democracy and tolerance that are the hallmarks of our way of life.

At the moment, I accept that association between them is loose. But it is hardening.

And the possibility of the two coming together – of terrorist groups in possession of WMD, even of a so-called dirty radiological bomb is now, in my judgement, a real and present danger.

And let us recall: what was shocking about September 11 was not just the slaughter of the innocent; but the knowledge that had the terrorists been able to, there would have been not 3,000 innocent dead, but 30,000 or 300,000 and the more the suffering, the greater the terrorists' rejoicing.

[About UN paralysis, the enforcing of Resolution 1441, fears of US unilateralism]

I accept fully that those opposed to this course of action share my detestation of Saddam. Who could not? Iraq is a wealthy country that in 1978, the year before Saddam seized power, was richer than Portugal or Malaysia.

Today it is impoverished, 60 per cent of its population dependent on food aid. Thousands of children die needlessly every year from lack of food and medicine. Four million people out of a population of just over twenty million are in exile.

The brutality of the repression – the death and torture camps, the barbaric prisons for political opponents, the routine beatings for anyone or their families suspected of disloyalty are well documented.

Just last week, someone slandering Saddam was tied to a lamp-post in a street in Baghdad, his tongue cut out, mutilated and left to bleed to death, as a warning to others.

I recall a few weeks ago talking to an Iraqi exile and saying to her that I understood how grim it must be under the lash of Saddam.

'But you don't,' she replied. 'You cannot. You do not know what it is like to live in perpetual fear.'

And she is right. We take our freedom for granted. But imagine not to be able to speak or discuss or debate or even question the society you live in. To see friends and family taken away and never daring to complain. To suffer the humility of failing courage in face of pitiless terror. That is how the Iraqi people live. Leave Saddam in place and that is how they will continue to live.

We must face the consequences of the actions we advocate. For me, that means all the dangers of war. But for others, opposed to this course, it means – let us be clear – that the Iraqi people, whose only true hope of liberation lies in the removal of Saddam, for them, the darkness will close back over them again; and he will be free to take his revenge upon those he must know wish him gone.

And if this house now demands that at this moment, faced with this threat from this regime, that British troops are pulled back, that we turn away at the point of reckoning, and that is what it means – what then?

What will Saddam feel? Strengthened beyond measure. What will the other states who tyrannise their people, the terrorists who threaten our existence, what will they take from that? That the will confronting them is decaying and feeble.

Who will celebrate and who will weep?

[About the implications of today's decision]

To retreat now, I believe, would put at hazard all that we hold dearest, turn the UN back into a talking shop, stifle the first steps of progress in the Middle East; leave the Iraqi people to the mercy of events on which we would have relinquished all power to influence for the better.

Tell our allies that at the very moment of action, at the very moment when they need our determination that Britain faltered.

I will not be party to such a course. This is not the time to falter. This is the time for this house, not just this government or indeed this prime minister, but for this house to give a lead, to show that we will stand up for what we know to be right, to show that we will confront the tyrannies and dictatorships and terrorists who put our way of life at risk, to show at the moment of decision that we have the courage to do the right thing.

I beg to move the motion.

18 March 2003 (www.publications.parliament.uk)

NOTES

The motion before the House of Commons that day was a long one, including 'that this House . . . therefore supports the decision of Her Majesty's Government that the United Kingdom should use all means necessary to ensure the disarmament of Iraq's weapons of mass destruction.'

The Prime Minister's speech was recognised as having gone a long way towards carrying the day for the Government. And yet he failed to convince 217 MPs, 139 of whom were from his own benches – the largest ever revolt against a Labour government.

Tony Blair deploys the main techniques of the persuasive speech (see Speech 29), namely to BED the audience through being believable, emotive and demanding. He makes every effort to be believable when linking Saddam's history of brutal dictatorship, territorial invasion and UN inspector evasion to the nightmare scenario of a WMD-armed dictator in league with a terrorist organisation – yet fails to convince us that even he really believes the link ('I accept that association between them is loose').

Blair's appeal to the emotions of his fellow MPs through the grotesque story of the unfortunate dissenter tied to a lamp-post and a discussion with an Iraqi exile is effective, but brief. The balance in the speech between fact-based analysis and emotion could well have been tilted more towards the latter.

Thirdly, Blair ends correctly with a demand for action, but it is hardly Churchillian. It starts well ('I will not be party to such a course') and deploys the technique of repetition important to an inspirational speech (see Speech 27), with 'this is the time for this house to show that . . . , to show that . . . , to show that . . . '

But it ends on a whimper – 'to show that at the moment of decision we have the courage to do the right thing'. Doing the right thing is rather a wishy-washy concept – and one already mentioned two clauses earlier. The speech calls for a conclusion more worthy of courage like: 'to show that at the moment of decision we have the courage to *fight for freedom, for justice and for the self defence of all peoples who dwell within range of the ruthless, amoral, evil dictator of Iraq*'.

The speech won the day, though whether that proved to be a fortuitous result is more open to debate.

PRISONER OF CONSCIENCE
by Vaughan Evans

Madame la Présidente, Mesdames et Messieurs, I 'ave always been a supporter of Amnesty Internationale. When I read of all zose political prisoners locked away in zeir evil cells, my 'eart bleeds for zem. But zere ees one political prisoner about 'oom Amnesty ees staying very quiet. *'Ees name ees Dominique Straus-Kahn* and 'e was until 'sree weeks ago ze next Président de La France.

'E is now incarcerated in an apartment in Manhattan, forced to wear an electronic tag. Zees ees a disgrace. 'E 'as 'ad one of ze most fundamental of French human rights taken away from 'eem: *ze right to séduce!*

Séduction ees a way of life in La France. It gives two great benefits to la société. Ze first ees ze social mobilité. In England, la société, it ees class-bound and rigid. In France, zat ees not so. A French businessman or politician will quite 'appily mix wiz a beautiful woman of any background or race. It ees ze same in Italy. Look at Signor Berlusconi – one of 'ees girlfriends, allegedly, ze one zat was une petit peu jeune, was a Muslim belly dancer. *Zat could not 'appen in England!*

Ze second great benefit of séduction ees *ze redistribution of wealz*. Americans are philansropists and zey give zeir monae away through zeir foundations. But ze English, zey are misers – zey squirrel zer monae away in zer tax 'aven colonies. We French are in between – we are generous wiz our monae, *we give it away to our maitresses!*

It was Dominique's great misfortune zat ze chambermaid in 'ees New York 'otel room *did not understand zees French concept of séduction*. But I am 'appy to say zat *'e 'as forgiven 'er!* Indeed as we speak 'is people are visiting zis lady's village en Afrique, allegedly, and, as long as she drops 'er charges, are offering one million dollars, allegedly, to 'elp wiz economic development!

Such générosité ees typical of ze man and of ze French. Mesdames et messieurs, s'il vous plaît, write to Amnesty Internationale and ask zem to campaign on be'alf of *zees tragically misunderstood gentilhomme, zees prisoner of conscience, zees séducteur honorable de la patrie!*

Madame la Présidente!

© Vaughan Evans, 2011

NOTES

This is of a somewhat different genre to the preceding persuasive speeches. Nevertheless, it sets out to be believable, emotive and demanding – to BED the audience (see Speech 29).

It is believable. It argues with conviction that the right to seduce is a fundamental human right in France, no less fundamental than liberty, equality and fraternity.

It is emotive. It stirs up the feelings of the audience as we perceive the wretched Dominique enchained with an electronic tag in a soulless, if luxurious, downtown apartment – and we admire his altruism as his people set off, allegedly, to transform the lives of African villagers.

And it is demanding. It ends with a call to action, to write to Amnesty International, deploying the power of three, reinforcing the perception of the victim, Dominique, as a gentleman, a prisoner of conscience and an honourable seducer.

How could you, dear reader, be anything but persuaded?!

EUROPE, ONE WINK AT A TIME
by Laura McCracken

[WHOLE SPEECH IN EXAGGERATED SOUTHERN US ACCENT] I am just a simple girl from Alabama. I grew up in a small town of 5,000 people called Enterprise – home of the boll weevil monument. We are the only city in the whole wide world with a monument to a bug! See, the boll weevil was an insect that came along and destroyed all our cotton crop, forcing us to diversify into . . . peanuts! Now we've got peanut butter, peanut brittle, peanut M&Ms . . . and, for some reason, millions of squirrels!

So I ask you, Mr Chairman, ladies and gentlemen, when you've got the boll weevil monument sitting in your very own back yard, why on earth would anyone want to mosey up to New York City to see the Statue of Liberty? Or fly all the way to Berlin to see the Eiffel Tower? [SHRUG]

Yet, despite my rich cultural heritage, I was itching to explore the rest of the world. So I found this ad for a ticket to Barcelona for just $199. Imagine me in Barcelona, just saying it makes you sound kinda glamorous, don't it? [WINK] After buying the ticket, I proceeded to the bookstore and bought every travel book I could find on . . . Italy. [SHAKE HEAD WITH REMORSE AND EMBARASSMENT] For those of you who aren't laughing, I suggest you refresh on your geography too!

So when I arrived in . . . Spain – thank you very much! – the immigration officer asked me why I was visiting 'Barthelona'. Well, I soon put him right on his pronunciation – and then told him about my little mix-up. He laughed so hard, that I felt a little humiliated. So I decided then and there to get some education about Europe. And for that I needed help . . .

My first lesson was Peter O'Shea. I thought that an Irishman would be a good starting point in my education, sort of Culture 101. After all they speak the same language, sort of. Now Peter, he taught me three things [WINK]: First, never drink before noon on a Sunday [CROSS

HEART]; second, if you hear that 'good craic' was had by all, don't alert the police; and third, the most important lesson of all, [PICK UP PINT OF GUINNESS] Guinness is indeed good for you! Slainte! [SWIG]

Having mastered Irish culture, I decided to up my game. His name was Benoit de Courtenay, a most sophisticated Parisian. He taught me about fashion [TIE LITTLE SCARF AROUND NECK WHILE CONTINUING TO SPEAK SLOWLY], poetry, philosophy, geography [WINK], champagne, gourmet cuisine and how to use a knife and fork! Did you know that the French even use them to eat fries? That's why they're called French fries! Santé, mon cheri! [SWIG]

And then came Claudio Palazzo, a Sicilian. Let me tell you, girls, the best thing about Italian men is that they love shoes even more than we do [HOLD UP PRADA SHOES]. And their appreciation of women doesn't stop at the feet [WINK]! But here's a lesson for y'all – even if he whispers the most beautiful words of love in your ear and makes you feel like you are the centre of the universe, never NEVER come between an Italian and his mother! Cin cin, bello! [SWIG, THEN GULP] Mama mia! See, I even learnt how to curse in Italian!

After my continental education, I headed back to more familiar territory [PUT ON 'AUDREY HEPBURN' ENGLISH HAT]. His name's Richard Garrett, an Englishman from the Home Counties. Stand up, honey. Let 'em take a look at you. [RICHARD STANDS UP BRIEFLY AND THEN SITS DOWN] Haven't I done well?! It's a good thing that the English have a sense of humour! [WINK] While Richard is never prone to whispering sweet words of love in the ear like Latin men, I knew that he 'fancied me' when he introduced me to his 'chums' in the pub. That's love! Cheers, mate! [SWIG]

Several years on in my education, I am proud to say that I have transformed myself from a 'simple girl from Alabama' to a 'woman of the world!' And I can say I love you in lots of languages . . . all except English, of course! But I learned one thing even more important – how to say, firmly but politely, again in many different languages, but especially in Italian, 'No, grazie!'

Mr Chairman

NOTES

I saw Laura perform this speech live at a contest a few years ago, if through clenched teeth – she beat me! She captivated the audience. Conjure up the wide-eyed naivety of Reese Witherspoon in *Legally Blonde*, add an extreme, Dolly Parton-esque country accent and an outrageous wink, and that was Laura on stage.

Obviously that effect cannot come through fully on the page. But there are hints, with the bracketed winks, swigs and gulps and the many asides to the audience, Miranda Hart-style, like 'when in arrived in . . . Spain – thank you very much' and, having embarrassed her latest amour, Richard, 'haven't I done well?' These and other engaging mannerisms kept the audience onside from beginning to end.

The speech has a lovely structure. The opening sets the scene graphically of this gal from Peanutsville, USA, curious to see the world. And the conclusion reminds us that by now she has not only seen it, but lived it. The body of the speech has a simple but effective structure, taking us seamlessly from Ireland to England, via France and Italy.

Let's try looking at the speech from the perspective of the tips on humorous speaking given earlier in this book (Speech 23), particularly the use of EET, namely embellish, extend and twist. Clearly the whole speech is one glorious embellishment, while the neat twist at the end of 'No, grazie' works well.

But the speech may well benefit from greater use of the second 'e', extension, namely when on a roll, keep rolling. The speech structure of four different countries/boyfriends makes for great variety within the time available, but gives less scope for extending an anecdote and milking the laughs. Indeed there could have been even less scope, since Laura's original draft contained a fifth boyfriend, a Spaniard who taught her the Flamenco dance of tragic love!

But a touch of ruthlessness can usually make any speech more humorous. In this case, Laura could have cut out another boyfriend, the one around whom the tales are not un-amusing, but the least amusing. She could then have focused on just three of them, giving her greater scope to extend a good line to get not just one, but two or three laughs on the trot.

But the speech works a treat as it is and remains one of the most memorable humorous speeches I have heard. Just one thing continues to niggle: why no Welshman?

A SALSA BROTH
by Vaughan Evans

The atmosphere is vibrant, the air cloying, the lights flashing, the bodies spinning, the salsa beat throbbing, repetitive and insistent. I want to dance. I am desperate to dance! *But how? And with whom?*

Mr Chairman, ladies and gentlemen, that was just four weeks ago and I was at the Casa de la Musica, a scenic open-air music space in the beautiful nineteenth-century town of Trinidad in Cuba. I was on a solo travelling holiday, family-free for the first time in twenty-five years. I wanted to dance but I didn't know how to dance salsa. I perched on a wall behind the band. *I was a genuine wallflower!*

Suddenly there was a big hi from my left. It was two young Dutch girls who I had helped out at the bus terminal in Havana three days earlier. They too were apprehensive about the salsa, so I suggested that we should all just get on the floor and give it a go. We did. My dance lasted about one minute. Two tall, super-cool, dreadlocked Cuban dudes descended onto our little group and *literally plucked the girls from me*. I was stranded there, like a prat, and had no option but to retreat to my wall. *I watched as the Dutch girls remained affixed to their captors for the rest of the evening – I consoled myself with the thought that this must be a mild form of Stockholm Syndrome!*

Time for some positive action, I thought. So the next day I signed up for a salsa class. I was taught the basic steps. Uno, dos, tres. Cinco, seis, siete. Uno, dos, tres. Cinco, seis, siete. Etc. Anything beyond that, like spinning your partner, was beyond me. But at least I had picked up the beat.

So that evening I returned to my spot on the wall and surveyed the scene. Soon I became aware of three Cuban women standing nearby, grooving to the music, one of whom was wearing the most outrageous denim hot pants. What the hell, I thought, nothing to lose. I went up to her: 'Quieres bailar, senorita?' Do you want to dance? Amazingly, she said OK, but she wanted a drink first. Fair enough, so we sat down and four mojitos duly arrived. She took her time, sipping her drink and chatting to her girlfriends, *completely ignoring me*. Finally she finished her drink, stood up, looked at me dismissively and said:

159

'Vamos,' let's go! Yeah, I thought, this is it, my moment of truth, my salsa initiation! She walked in front of me towards the dance floor – and *kept on going, straight past the dance floor and towards the exit!* I caught up with her. 'Hey, donde vamos?', I asked, where are we going? She looked at me as if I were an imbecile. *'Tu casa,' she replied, your place!* Oops, I think I might have *misinterpreted the intended nature of the relationship.* Back to square one. *Back to my wall.*

I returned to the Casa de la Musica on the next, my final night. I sat on my wall for a couple of hours, *resigned to my fate.* I watched the bands and the dancing, enjoying the music, making no attempt to dance. With half an hour to go, I went to the bar and ordered one last mojito, one for the road, and while I was waiting there the cook came out of the kitchen, grooving to the music. She was in her late sixties, dark face, dark Afro speckled with white, dressed in a pink uniform, with white collar, white cuffs and white apron. She had a huge, pendulous chest and an even larger rump. She was indeed completely spherical, *but she was managing to move the whole ensemble bang on time to the beat!* Before I knew it I came out with: *'Senora, quieres bailar?'* She looked at me as if I was some kind of a nutter and then burst into a huge grin: *'Porque non?!' Why not?!* We walked down to the heaving dance floor, found a space, which she widened in no time *through the judicious use of her lethal backside.*

Ladies and gentlemen, that dance was half an hour of pure joy, a taste of heaven. It more than made up for the preceding eleven and a half hours of purgatory. They say that too many cooks spoil the broth, but let me tell you this: *this Cuban cook served up a sensational salsa broth!*

Mr Chairman

© Vaughan Evans, 2014

NOTES

This speech is a romp. It is effectively just the one rollicking story, with no attempt at moralising but with simple exploitation of the strand of British humour that is self-deprecation.

It is based loosely on a genuine fortnight's holiday in Cuba by the speaker, but with a series of unconnected events rolled into one semi-fictitious continuum. The grooving cook, for example, exists, but was spotted and indeed briefly conversed with, if not danced with, at another bar in another town!

Applying the EET tips (see Speech 23), the speech is indeed embellished, as described above; there is some extension, as with the series of lines culminating in the gag on Stockholm Syndrome; and it ends with a twist on the well-known proverb about too many cooks – a tad contrived, perhaps, but, in the immortal words of Joe E. Brown to Jack Lemmon, 'Nobody's perfect'!

PS This Humorous Speech II slot was originally designated to be one by my fellow club member, Aileen Bennett, which won the UK and Ireland Humorous Speech Contest in 2001. It was called 'Does this speech make me look fat?' and was a riot of self-deprecating hilarity, one of the funniest I have heard anywhere. It kick-started Aileen's career as a motivational speaker when she migrated to Louisiana. But it turns out that her copy of the speech has been lost – probably somewhere mid-Atlantic – and it was never recorded. A shame for her, and for the world at large, but a chance for me to nip in with my Cuban saga . . . !

PPS It is curious that both the speeches I originally wanted as exemplars of humorous speaking, as well as that for the tall tale (next up), were created and delivered by women. This wasn't deliberate, but may unwittingly reflect a trend observed nationally. A few years ago nearly all comedians on the circuit and on the telly were male – the exceptions being the likes of Dawn French, Jennifer Saunders or Catherine Tate (with her gloriously obscene creation, Nan). These days there are many more – indeed many (most?) of the sell-out shows on the Edinburgh Fringe over the last few years have been of female comics, with the likes of Sara Pascoe, Felicity Ward and Luisa Omielan (with her infectious 'What would Beyoncé do?') raising the rafters. One theory, well, mine, is that female comics can these days get away with telling outrageous (and grossly embellished) stories of their conquests, while men doing likewise (imagine *Men Behaving Badly* being shown on TV today?!) get labelled misogynistic. That's OK – it's time we blokes cleaned up our act, and anyway, we rather enjoy listening to sexist comediennes!

APPENDIX 6:
A TALL TALE SPEECH

FRUITY COCKTAILS
by Sonia Aste

Madam Chairman, ladies and gentlemen – mid-life crisis! It hits you like a slap in the face [TURN ROUND 360 DEGREES WHILE SLAPPING FACE]

Oh no, I'm getting old! Have any of you felt the same? Yeah, a couple of hands are up. One or two of you still have your hands down – in denial! There's no need! Don't worry, because there are three simple solutions:

- First – get a young lover! Yeah, I know, a bit of a hassle . . .
- Second – buy the red PORSCHE – brrrmmm, brrrmmm – but expensive . . .
- Third – and the one I opted for: get the boob job!

Not everyone approved of the idea. My mother threw her arms in the air: 'Mi hijita, my little daughter, how can you do this to yourself? Do you have no self-esteem?' Uhhh . . . no! 'Didn't I teach you that it's the beauty on the inside that counts?' I had to break it to my mother that I'm not that pretty on the inside either. So I might as well fake it likewise on the outside!

Off I went to Harley Street and my appointment with Dr Maximiliano – Mexican, tall, veeeery handsome! [MEXICAN ACCENT] 'Señora, shall we take our top off?' I'm going like 'yeah!' – but he was talking posh and only meant me!

As I am taking my blouse off, he brings in an enormous basket of fruit. 'Señora, here we do things the tropical way. I will fit you with the fruit that is right for your breast size. Do you want the size of an apple – or a grapefruit?'

'Well, doctor,' I reply indignantly, 'seeing that I'm already the size of an orange . . . ' 'Ah, no, Señora, I'm afraid not,' he kindly points out, 'With respect, you are, shall we say, lime size. Squashed lime.'

Squashed lime? Moi?

I grab a couple of grapefruits and try them on for size. No. Not big enough. I try some honeydew melons? Better. How about these watermelons? Yeah! Now we're talking!

Two weeks later I emerge from the surgery, accompanied by my watermelons. Or, rather, preceded by them. For once I had to thank my Pilates classes because I have never needed to work more on my core balance [CLOWN AROUND, TOP-HEAVY, WALKING OFF-BALANCE]. But soon I get the gist of it and I'm feeling great.

In fact I have never felt better! For the first time in my life, I stand out in the crowd. Walking in the street, passers-by turn to stare and bump into each other. When I give a presentation at work, my colleagues no longer gaze out of the window. At cocktail parties, my companions are spellbound – they can't take their eyes off me. Well, to be precise, off my watermelons . . .

It was the shallow life I had always dreamed of! I am like a Latina Dolly Parton! But it couldn't last. The watermelons, like all fruit, ripened, matured and eventually exploded . . .

I was rushed in for an emergency procedure. My watermelons were extracted and with them two litres of sweet watermelon juice – which I later learned the doctors and nurses had mixed with rum and grenadine syrup to make a delicious rum punch. Salud!

I soon recovered, but I'm finished with that cosmetic stuff. Back to my mid-life crisis, back to my original fruit size. One thing I have learned though, and I'll share it with you, is this.

If life gives you squashed limes, you're gonna have to make margaritas.

Madam Chairman

© Sonia Aste, 2010

NOTES

I heard Sonia deliver this tall tale live. It was utterly captivating. It ticked every box in the tall tale to-do list – and more.

A tall tale needs to be credibly incredible, organised and deadpan, or COD (see Speech 26). At the start we wondered how Sonia could possibly have had a boob job, because there she was standing in front of us with not a huge amount there – well, more than crushed limes, as the doctor opined rather cruelly, more like Sonia's perceived oranges – well, mandarin oranges . . . ! But finally we learnt that the procedure had had to be reversed, so the story was credible after all!

The speech was superbly organised – setting the scene with the mid-life crisis, describing life with the watermelons and then the twist – their explosion! And it was delivered deadpan throughout – as if we were being let in on a very sorry, personal tale.

It also ticked one of the most important boxes in humorous speaking (see Speech 23). It was as self-deprecating as you can get.

One area where the speech might have been improved is in the ending. It was in fact a clever extension of the watermelon juice for rum punch theme, but that might not have been obvious to all. The conclusion is the last thing that people remember from a speech, so it has to be the best.

And it is usually unwise to make the audience work too hard to think about what a conclusion means. What may look good on paper can be lost when spoken live.

That said, this was a tall tale to savour – one to take with a pinch of mint leaf, a slug of Havana Club and, yes, a couple of squashed limes – and toast with a mojito!

APPENDIX 7:
AN IMPROMPTU SPEECH

IS MONEY THE ROOT OF ALL EVIL?
by Bill Russell

That's a difficult question for a banker.

But, Madam Chairman, ladies and gentlemen, let me ask you this. Is it evil for you to want a raise at work so that you can afford a bigger home, better schooling for your children or a vacation for your family? Is it evil to want to secure a better future for you and your family?

Money is not evil if used properly and if we have a respect for it. We all expect to get paid for our jobs and wouldn't feel 'evil' in asking for a raise or receiving one for work well done.

When Mother Teresa asks us to donate money are we funding evil? Is she evil for asking for it? Of course not. Money in the right hands can do so many wonderful things and the works of Mother Teresa and other charities are testament to that. Money does not corrupt good people. There are those that love money for money's sake and that is dangerous – and, yes, potentially evil.

But, for most of us, money is simply a currency, a means of improving our lives – and the lives of others.

Madam Chairman

© Bill Russell, 1999

NOTES

This speech was delivered some time ago and as it was impromptu was not written down. Bill spoke for the full two and a half minutes, as stipulated in the contest, but the above accounts for only about a minute and a half of that. It is all that Bill can recall, but is enough to show how it won him the Britain and Ireland impromptu speaking championship that year.

Bill is a larger-than-life character. The Chicagoan owns the stage, dominates the room and carries immense power and range in his voice. He has since become a stand-up comedian.

Thus the power of this speech came partly from the audience anticipating some good laughs from a known humorous speaker and then being delivered something quite different. Two years earlier he had also made it to the finals and had to address the topic 'Is it better to be smart or good-looking?' He chose the latter, because it enabled him to reel off a stream of gags on the theme. He had the audience in fits, but didn't win – because they, and he in reality, believed it better to be smart.

Two years on, in the speech above, he started off in familiar mode, in mock outrage that a banker should be asked such a question – he was indeed at the time a derivatives trader. The audience looked forward to be being treated to some insider juice and jokes on the evils of investment banking.

Not at all – he treated the subject seriously and personally, relating the desire for money to the natural human instinct to do the best for the family. He even brought in, for a speech delivered in mainly Catholic Ireland, as Yvonne did in Appendix 2, the Catholic icon of Mother Teresa.

Smart always beats good-looking.

THE
IMPRVEMENT
ZONE

Looking for life inspiration?

The Improvement Zone has it all, from **expert advice** on how to advance your **career** and boost your **business**, to improving your **relationships**, revitalising your **health** and developing your **mind**.

Whatever your goals, head to our website now.

www.improvementzone.co.uk

INSPIRATION ON THE MOVE

INSPIRATION DIRECT TO YOUR INBOX